CW0070£322

This book is funded by the insurance money.

Dedicated to my dearest mother.

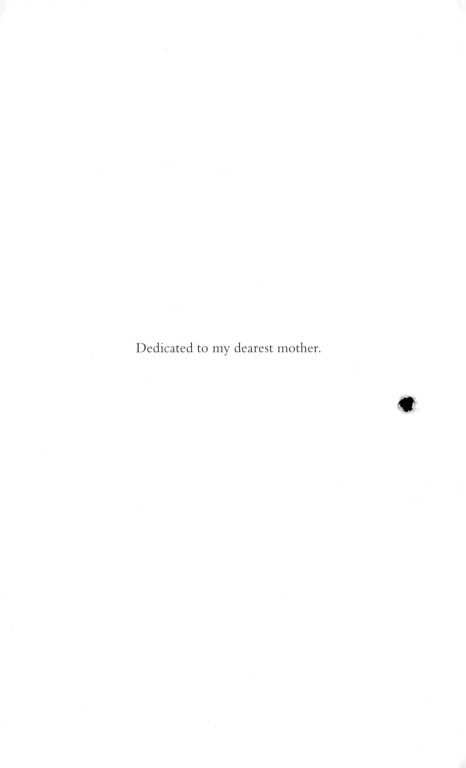

A Life in Film & Bromsgrove

WESLEY HENRY

(ACTOR / WRITER / FILMMAKER / ODD JOB MAN /
LIST MAKER / DEPRESSIVE / DIVORCEE)

CONTENTS

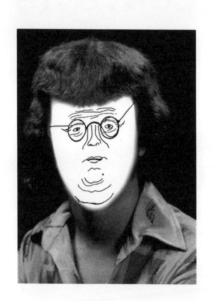

There is a beautiful world out there, so I have heard. My name is Wesley Henry and I am hoping for a break. I am just a man but I have a dream and I won't rest until I wake up rich and famous and sexy. Sure, I miss my old house and my old wife, but now I am all by myself I can focus on my acting career without any superfluous distractions.

This book is a portfolio of my acting and writing, with some photographs and other stuff chucked in to make it slightly less boring. I mainly only ever act in my own films and dramas because I have my own artistic vision and no one else has ever really showed much interest. However, I would like to get on the TV now though so am available for all jobs in this area (Bromsgrove, Redditch, Droitwich Spa).

1.

ALL ABOUT ME

Introduction

I was born in Bromsgrove in 1969. It was a prolonged and painful labour for my mom and she has held it against me ever since. I don't have a Dad as I was conceived via a funfair. I can remember being twelve months old and having a photograph taken in the kitchen sink at my nan's house; this was the last time I smiled or felt truly happy. I am a deep thinker and an active member of the *Hollyoaks* Facebook page.

My acting heroes are Robert Powell in *The Detectives* and Jack Osborne from *Hollyoaks*. I also admire Nick Owen and Shefali Oza from *Midlands Today* for their presenting skills and enduring optimism in the face of non-stop bad news.

I have always been interested in film and television. I worked in the Bromsgrove Blockbuster Video for half a decade, and my first wedding had an *Aladdin* theme. This, in truth, was a very unhappy marriage due to my wife's serial philandering. She was vindictive and unkind and deliberately slept with men who had the same first names as my heroes in a sick attempt to dampen my already limited enjoyment of life. I have got into acting for two reasons;

One:
To prove my ex-wife and her life coach wrong.

Two:
A lady in IKEA said I had the ideal sized head for television.

Statistics, experience and my GCSE results would indicate that I am not a genius, but I think with some work I could well be. My ambitions are massive and my talent knows no bounds.

Thanks to countless years of strife, my acting performances have an emotional depth that draw upon real life despair and beat those of meat head actors like Sylvester Stallone or Grant Mitchell hands down. Since my wife left me for a brick shit-house, I have lost all respect for muscle-bound men, but one day I will be bigger than them and have a better car, and she will be sick to her stomach. Although my body at the moment is a little under developed I can beef up if a roll dictates it. I am on a fitness plan to get buff by Christmas 2013, but my ass is already very firm in places.

I am a fully rounded individual, part-time odd job man and I sometimes do a lot of work for charity. After my divorce, I did partially pierce my left tit but apart from that I have no other body art.

Wesley Henry
Bromsgrove, 2013

A computer realisation of how I intend to look in six months. //   3

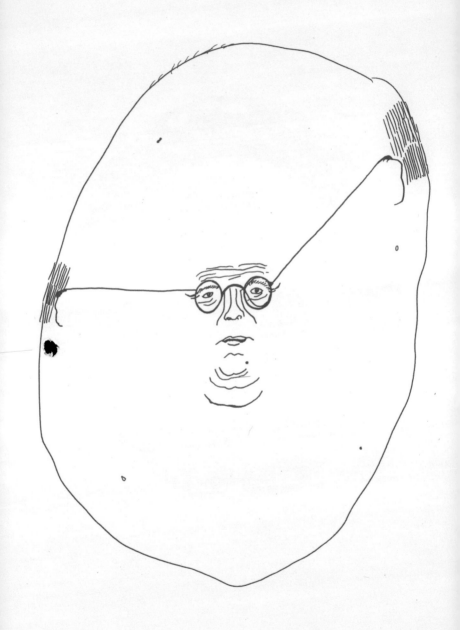

//*An artist's impression of my current head.*

Personal Details

Age: 43 years.

Nationality: British.

Body Type: Disappointing.

Health: Up and down.

Height: 5'7".

Eye Colour: Green / murky brown.

Weight: 14st *plus*.

Head to Screen Ratio: Perfect.

Location: Bromsgrove.

Hair Colour: 26 strands of fine black hair, greying.

Playing Age: 18–60 years.

Role Types: Victims of circumstance.

Accents & Dialects: Bromsgrove, Redditch.

Voice Character: Broken man.

Voice Quality: Dull / insipid.

Languages: English, regret.

Disabilities: Cannot drive.

Special Skills

Martial arts, boxing, extreme stunts, combat fighting, horse riding, cycling, rock climbing, ten-pin bowling, crying, Jenga.

Accolades

Bronze level attendance certificate for half a term at Lil' Tykes After School Club, Catshill. GCSE results also available on request (performance somewhat affected by a dicky tummy).

Potential Roles

I am not daft, I know I am not the best looking 43 year old in my close, but Smeggy Dave's sunbathing will catch up with him someday. Still, I try to look after myself as best as I can between my off days, and can bend myself into any role, act or four door saloon. To say I have a way with women would be a lie, but I have read quite a few books about them so am well versed in the various ways a man can ensnare a beautiful lady. My calamitous love life does also enable me to be able to cry real tears on demand and upon the drop of a hat. With such experience, I feel I have it within my capabilities to play any put upon man or victim of an unfaithful spouse with aplomb; psychopath is also well within my range.

Styling Requirements

Let's be realistic, I am bald, I have a big head and I am no great shakes in the trouser department. Big deal, take a little look at yourself before you start judging me. I can wear a wig, listen to a Paul McKenna tape and fashion suitable outfits to distract from my flaws. The fact is you TV makers need more people like me on the box. Why? My head is the perfect ratio for TV; I have had it verified. Now, I know I may appear like a rough diamond offscreen, but with the correct styling I can light up any television. Styling can make or break a man, so if you plan on hiring me I would insist on some input on the characters wardrobe. I need bold colours or tight checks to ensure maximum wow effect and distract viewers from the imbalance in my head to body ratio. Have you ever seen a man strobe in real life? No, well let me live my dream and treat everyone else to some unforgettable television.

Sex Scenes

I am hypersensitive in the bedroom so would prefer to wear numerous pairs of pants to build up some layer of defence between myself and said lover, both for my own insurance and the good of the whole crew. Sadly, my ex-wife really blurred the line between lovemaking and emotional degradation, so from now on I would also insist that there is no sniggering on set.

Privates, we all have them. Some big, some small and some normal. Let me tell you where I stand. I will do naked from the top half up if the filming is done tastefully. As to where the top half begins there is much debate, some say hip bone, some say pubes, I say clavicle.

I must say now I will only do lovemaking scenes not sex-fests. Same thing? On this point only, I must agree with my ex-wife and her car park pals and say no; sex and lovemaking are not the same thing. I will not be pounded, I will not be bent over, and I will not do anything in a sports hall or outdoor venue. Scenes must all be carried out in the safety of a bed (preferably marital) with lights dimmed, if not fully turned off. I would also like to be in a stable relationship with any actress before going to bed with her in any film. Additionally, I should mention that I am liable to chapped lips and cold sores.

Goody or Baddy

I won't say I will only play goodies, but I would prefer the ratio to be somewhere around 80:20 in favour of the nice guy. I am mindful that I don't want to get typecast as a wrong'un because I had that crap all through High School and no matter what they say, that shit sticks. It has taken me years to shake off people's shoddy opinions about me so I don't want to undo all my hard work by playing the local nonce in some two-bit daytime drama.

I refuse to play the part of a paedophile, sex attacker or life coach, all are degenerative scumbags. I will play murderers (conditional), arsonists, fraudulent accountants, alcoholics, drug fiends (preferably recovered / relapsed), fly tippers and scrap metal thieves.

Exceptions:
Spielberg; I would play a pervert for Spielberg if it got my name on the poster.

People I refuse to work with:
I refuse to work with any of the following people, each for differing reasons.

Nicolas Cage
Gabriel Clarke
Cheryl Cole
Quentin Wilson
Any life coach

Casting agents please note, Paul McKenna is not a life coach, he is a hypnotist and self-improvement author. Some days, I do also believe him to be the second coming of Christ. Whilst on the subject, I would also like to make it known that I will play any religion, but refuse to read up around the subject.

Here follows a full breakdown of my acting / odd job price list, a full mental breakdown actually being one of my specialities.

What You Get for Your Money

£15   Blow up one bag of medium sized party balloons by mouth. (No machines.)

£30   Inspect your guttering and re-enact one of three key scenes from the kid's animated movie Shrek.

£35   List three items on eBay in the style of your favourite character from movie history. (Price + 10% of the final sale profit.)

£40   Play a supporting role in a local production + carry out your full weekly shop in period costume.

£45   Bleed radiators as Martin Clunes / Jeremy Guscott / Halle Berry. Or, full PC virus and spyware removal + 40 point MOT PC tune up and hardware upgrade advice. (Most popular package.)

£50   Full PAT tests on up to five electrical items + one flat pack furniture assembly and a guaranteed five follows on Twitter (including Rick Edwards).

£80   Theatrical performance of a Shakespeare monologue + taking responsibility for traffic / speeding offences.

£150   Night club appearance package.* (Subject to stipulations, see next page.)

£200   Ten hours private detective / honey trap work in the style of renowned Hollywood actor Keanu Reeves. (Price not dependent on success rate.)

£250   Play a leading man role depicting a generally respec-
ted member of society in a choice of two accents †
+ complete Angry Birds on your mobile device.
(Including all stars and golden eggs + £9.99.)

£400   Panic attack.

£500   Full emotional breakdown. (Charges cover following month spent in bed, medication and therapy.)

£1000   Arsonist.

£2000   Sex pest. (Spielberg dependent.) ‡

* I not only offer public appearances but also join up as a fully
functioning member of the bar or door staff. I will perform
all roles within a club or pub except glass collecting and toilet
duties. I will not perform public appearances at what was Fuse
Night Club, Redditch or Euphoria in Bromsgrove for a variety
of personal reasons.

† No actor on television or film has ever passed off a convin-
cing Redditch or Bromsgrove accent; that is a fact. I can do
both and will bring my own brand of torment to each accent
in any role that does or does not require it.

‡ It is a sorry state of affairs that I have to say the listed fees for
'arsonist' and 'sex pest' are to play those characters in a production only and involve no real life criminal activity. Spielberg
or no Spielberg.

All jobs come with complimentary weeping.

Noel Edmonds' Tears

As I mentioned earlier, I have the undoubted talent of being able to cry on demand whenever or wherever I am called upon to do so. Luckily for me, the crying is drawn from a deep well of sadness that sits right at the very core of my being and taps upon past heart-breaks, deception and rejection.

Ever seen Noel Edmonds cry? Course you have, but have you ever seen him do it sincerely? No. I spend every waking hour walking the tight rope of tears, feeling like I may cry at any time for no reason. When Edmonds cries on *Deal or No Deal* he cries as a multi-millionaire who happily drives home in the bus lane in his custom made taxi humming his favourite tune. When I cry you know you are getting the real deal. After a crying scene I don't leave set to go back to my mansion. I go back to my nan's terrace house with an abiding sadness which leaves me bed stricken for days. Authentic from the heart despair is my calling card, so don't let any other actor / presenter fob you off with phony crocodile emotion.

Training in Woe

I received no formal training as an actor, although I did attend an evening drama / support club for three weeks in 2004 on the advice of my local doctor. This preluding the full thrust of my marital problems, I didn't cotton on at the time that Dr. Darius had only sent me to the class so he could pay my then wife one of his 'home visits'. Anyway, the fourth week's empathy session was cancelled due to lack of interest so I arrived home sooner than expected. I walked through the front door to find my GP doing ungodly things to Shelly with the broken DVD zapper from the lounge. I never went back to the drama class after that day, in fact, I didn't leave the house for a month.

To be honest, I don't believe you can ever be trained to feel emotions, you need to put yourself through the mill to find full truth in your performances. You do not get to my stage in proceedings (with a failed marriage, disappointing career, shattered hopes and suicidal leanings) without an acutely rich understanding of emotions and the harsh lessons of life. In this sense, I have practiced and trained for 43 years for every role I take on. Trust me, I know how to act as if my whole world is crumbling around me, Christ I am not even acting. I often hear Hollywood actors talking about taking months to get into the mindset of manic depressives and I don't know whether to laugh or cry. I'm sure if they shot these movies in Bromsgrove people would find their motivation a lot quicker.

Representation

I am represented by local entrepreneur and dickhead, Jonny Sheaths. Jonny has me opening scrap yards and handing out condoms in night clubs. He says these are celebrity appearances, but, in all honesty, I am at the dump most weekday mornings and the guys can't get in unless I'm there as I have the only set of keys.

I cannot get across just quite how much of a scumbag the man is, yet like in my marriage, I am working off the theory that it is best to keep your friends close but your enemies closer. Jonny is well connected in Redditch and Bromsgrove and I cannot afford anyone better, plus he sometimes lets me sleep in his portakabin.

References

Mr. Jonny Sheaths, Agent

Acting is all in the eyes and there is only so much cheating make-up can do. The only way to get the official 'haven't slept in months' look is to do just that. Nothing shines out from the silver screen more than a person who has slept well the night before. Sure, that's fine if you're playing some Billy Bubblegum choirboy, but if that is not the case then you can't go on living the life of bloody Riley and expect the shitbags at home to feel your pain. You need to get real, avoid sleep, knock yourself about a bit and stop getting blow jobs too, it lacks professional integrity. This ain't *Disneyland* folks.

When I first met Wesley he seemed, from the outside, to have everything. He was married and sang karaoke down his local every Friday night. He could carry a tune okay, but don't get me wrong, he was nothing special even just in the Bromsgrove karaoke scene. I offered to take Wesley onto my books and promised to make him a star. Within a month I had rekindled my twelve year affair with his wife, swindled him out of fifty grand and put an extra layer of aching pain in his heart. I gave him all this and now he is a shadow of the man he once was but twice the actor.

I knew singing wasn't Wesley's destiny, but I spotted a true acting talent lurking beneath his flabby jacket potato exterior. Even before I ruined his life Wesley was no happy clapper, but now I have etched a true despair in his psyche and unlocked a brooding volcano of sadness in his soul. Sure our work relationship is a little rocky now, but deep inside Wesley knows I have paved his way to success. All he has to do now is keep his head down and check his ex-wife's Facebook updates daily.

To surmise ~~officer,~~ I can assure you that ~~Carla Powers~~ Wesley Henry is a well balanced, outstanding individual ~~and a truly gifted masseuse.~~

Tomy Sheaths

10.1.2013

Jane Thompson, Mom's Friend

Wesley is a good boy. He is very quiet, sensitive and absolutely no trouble, most of the time. Over the past forty years, I have watched him blossom into a lovely chap with few blips on the way and only a slight tailing off in recent times.

Since the dissolution of his marriage, Wesley has cut a rather crestfallen figure around his mother's house. I therefore urge you to give him any opportunity possible to re-establish his wavering confidence and get him out and about a bit more.

I must add my recommendation does not come without a few reservations. Wesley has always had a tendency to be somewhat overwhelmed by the day-to-day rigours of life and can often suffer at the hands of some of the more boisterous bigger boys. When hiring Wesley, one would be wise to be a little wary of overloading his plate as his mother assures me she could not go through another six months like she just had with him. With this in mind, perhaps consider giving him a role as some form of background scenery or human prop to start with and take it from there.

Jane Thompson

14.1.2013

How I might look as a background painting in a TV pub. //

The Television Star: Over the following few pages I have mocked up a few images of some roles I think I could play really well. First off, this is what I might look like on the television / inside a broken CRT monitor.

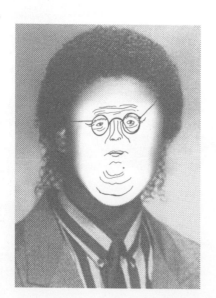

The Hirsute Pop Star: We all know the best pop stars are troubled and hirsute. I may be very bald now, but this photo shows just how well I can pull hair off, afro or otherwise.

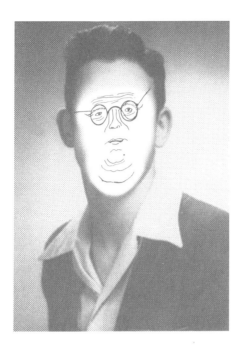

The Fifties Movie Star: This picture proves nothing other than the fact I belong on the big screen. The 1950's is an era my face would have thrived in. I really do believe if I had been around then everything would have been fine.

The Fat ****** :
I'm not a memorably fat man, but if a role did require me to pile on the pounds I have all the tools necessary to let myself go a bit and make the leap over to morbid obesity with relative ease. As earlier stated, I would refuse to get my tits out though.

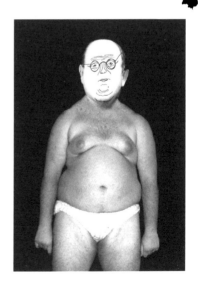

17

The Fallen: The injured or infirm. Broken bones or spirit,
I am your walking wounded, I am your out-patient.

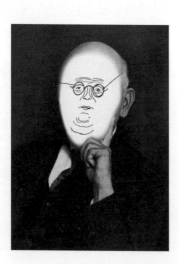

The Bald and Rich:
A lot of people say money
doesn't make you happy,
so I could probably have
a stab at playing a rich
man. 'More money, more
problems', sure, but less
sleeping on office porta-
kabin floors.

The Sleepy: Put me in a dressing gown and you have found my natural domain, like Lionel Messi with a football at his feet or Picasso with a paintbrush in his hand. Come into my office the door is open, I am sleeping on the floor.

The Trapped: I spent many a year stuck under a large unmovable object. To turn professional at it would be the biggest two fingers up to my ex-wife imaginable.

The Bendy: Bent in two from athletic ability, bent in two by regret. You say potato, I say topical haemorrhoid cream. Ain't no man alive with such low self-esteem to have spent more days up his own ass than me, plus I can act at all 360 degrees.

The Prom King: That's right it's an olden days prom night photograph from America. And look that's my face in the frame to prove even though I am now in my forties I could still play an eighteen year old school leaver, no problem. Obviously, the kid would have to have some kind of condition or had a proper shit life, i.e. BAFTA territory.

A Big Chap with a Bow Tie: The thing I want to get across here is that I can do comedy. *The Nutty Professor, Big Momma's House,* all that stuff. I mean I'm not personally much of a fan of people point blank laughing at me, but I would pick up the cheque nevertheless.

The Man in the Dark: A man alone in a dark room. Down beat, low key. Quite sad. Piece of piss.

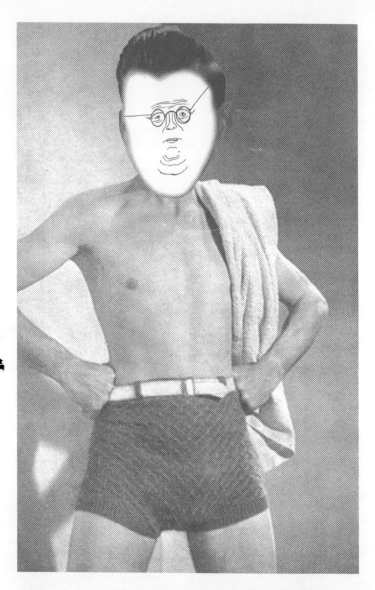

Man in Pants: Providing the film is artfully shot, I am willing
to play a character with venereal disease.

// The above image is for Steven Spielberg's eyes only.

Social Network / Fan Base

Lack of friends in the real world has not prevented me from forging on with my online social network. Indeed, at this very moment, across all platforms I have a ready-made audience of around twenty friends; almost fourfold the number of my real life dependable amount. Even more impressive is the fact that amongst this online number are two bona fide celebs, meaning 10% of my online friends are celebrities.

When my ex-wife left me, like most other things, our mutual friends were not split entirely equally between the two of us. To help determine the allotment of the group Shelly devised a winner takes all system, by which she set up a questionnaire on each of our Facebook pages asking each person who they preferred, her or me. Whoever got the highest percentage of votes between us got to keep all the friends as their own, and the other poor sod had to sever all ties.

Needless to say, Shelly won the vote by 97% as she was having sex with most of the friendship group at the time. In total, I secured three votes, one from me, one from my mom and the other one I can only assume was a misclick. After I lost all my online friends, I spent a couple of three weekends on the trot inconsolably adding anybody and everybody I did or did not like the look of. Anyway, now any talk of restraining orders has long since past, I am currently followed by none other than Kinga from *Big Brother* (the one who got lodged on a bottle of Lambrini) and Rick (pedigree specimen) Edwards off *T4*.

I feel all the better thinking that the terrible sadness I went through has led me to the friendship of the truly great and good. The closest Shelly has ever come to stardom with her new bag of bollocks was when he was featured on BBC *Rogue Traders* for selling his bogus protein shakes out the back of his Vectra; it truly was the best phone call I have ever made.

Violence

My mom and I attend self-defence classes up to twice a month at the local community centre, where I have learned how to conquer my natural balance issues and use my inner strength to throw down both young moms and elderly ladies.

If the right role came up, in which I was required to take part in a violent exchange, I would need to run all activities by my mother first. The atmosphere of combat leaves me prone to vomiting and heightens my already often profuse sweating. After my last fight I cried for four months straight. To this day I still lay awake for nights on end seeing life coaches in the shadows, my body keeled over, sodden in the foetal position, vomiting into the nearest bin. I have since made a vow, both to myself and my mom, that I will not put myself through this trauma again for anything less than £200.

Reliability

No matter what you may have heard, I can assure you that I am very reliable and you can depend on me 100%. For example, if you were ever to ask me to be on set at 9 a.m. then I would make sure to be there at 8.45 a.m. This is exactly the kind of thing that matches my skillset perfectly, you don't have to worry about that. Obviously, problems can occur, as I am yet to pass my driving test, meaning that I am fully reliant on my mother and passing strangers if public transport should fail me. Assuming everything goes okay getting into work though, fingers crossed, I promise you won't have any bother with me.

Aside from acting, if you ever have any sort of problem with your computer I will be able to fix it. I do also carry a blue biro about my person at all times, so you are more than welcome to borrow that should you need it. Recently, I have also flirted with the idea of buying a packet of Polo's at the start of each day, so if you ever want one, all you have to do is ask. All in all, whatever you are looking for, I am your man. Whether it's acting, writing or just something to freshen your breath in a morning, you need not look any further than me.

Employment History

On first inspection, my past employment record (see p.28) may seem like a somewhat scattergun approach to launching a film career. However, I can assure you that I have seen each and every job as a stepping stone to future stardom. In essence, I have spent a long time finding out what I don't want to do, and that is everything I have done before, and now I am ready for international recognition and success.

I have a valuable range of experience across various sectors, including the movie business (Blockbuster Video) and I still have many uniforms left over from previous jobs that could be well utilised in acting roles. Yes, CV-wise, there may well be certain yearlong gaps and other breaks somewhat sporadic in nature, but this does not mean anything. Some people take the odd gap year to travel the world after university, I took mine a few decades later and stayed more local. Big deal.

Employment

Bromsgrove Rovers Catering Van / Clamping Co.
Four months.

I managed to work here for about four months before I suffered a humiliating half-time sacking over the Tannoy system. The Rovers were playing Ford Sports Daventry in the second round of the FA Vase in front of 301 people. Someone got hospitalized off some dodgy beef and I carried the can. Wounded.

Blockbuster Video
Five years, discounting a six month sick period.

I lost my job in the layoffs following the introduction of the drop-off bin. It really hit me hard and I now cherish the time I had there. I guiltlessly watched free films all day and got to know where so many people lived. Ultimately though it was a crushing blow to realise I could not compete with a bin.

Flawed Floors, Door Mat Man
Can't quite remember the exact dates.

Post-divorce venture, selling second-hand, reclaimed flooring, mainly from my marital home. Things went well initially but stock soon ran dry. I was having to get stuff from B&Q, put a bit of a mark-up on top and sell it on. People quickly got wise to what I was doing. Shame, I did really quite enjoy this job.

(Four year barren spell.)

Date@8 Online Dating Agency
Three months, roughly, on and off.

An online dating service for men in the Midlands who looked better eight years ago and women whose standards have dropped a little and vice versa. Part founder / part lonely heart.

Multi-Dimensional Actor / Odd Job Man
Ongoing / dormant.
The first odd job man in Bromsgrove to offer big screen movie tie-ins to all their labour, allowing customers both a unique and cheap opportunity to support their local movie star (see p.20).

(*Six month sabbatical / black hole.*)

Other Paid Work

Part Time Food and Beverage Associate
My job here was to be treated like a piece of shit until 4 a.m. in the morning.

Factory Worker
During my younger days. The staff were all middle-aged and took great satisfaction in deriding those who still had their whole lives ahead of them. Luckily enough, they always left me alone for some reason.

Telesales Operative
I had to phone people up to say their car insurance was due for renewal. Unfortunately, I got the sack because I kept leaving my home number on the answer machines by mistake.

Part Time Insurance Clerk
Not really sure what I was meant to be doing here. I used to walk home at lunch so I could have a cry.

Freelance Grandson
Duties include opening and closing loft doors, full facial food removal and operating as a human draft excluder.

Unpaid Work

I have a rich knowledge and understanding of working for nothing. Since hiring my agent, Mr. Jonny Sheaths, I have performed a plethora of jobs for him, each for absolutely sod all.

In January 2009, Mr. Sheaths had an old Austin Metro with a faulty hydraulic boot. My job was to sit in the back and hold the boot down until the journey was concluded. Upon stopping, Jonny would then press a blank button on the dashboard at which time I had to release the boot and make a high pitched pipping sound.

For the past five years, I have also dutifully recorded *Match of the Day* every Saturday and then cut all the bullshit out so that Jonny can just see the goals. Day-to-day the electrics in Jonny's portakabin are always tripping, my job then is to go and flip the switches back on whilst avoiding banging my head on all the things he is throwing at me. In my time I have also had to:

- Attach photos to emails, scan and photocopy things.

- Answer the phone in a female voice.

- Unblock the toilet / shut the fucking door.

- Catch the bus to the family planning clinic and get a big bag of free NHS condoms.

- Carefully remove condoms out of packets and place them into Jonny's own branded foil wraps.

- Mop up fluids.

Me (left) and Jonny Sheaths (right) in bushes, with company. //   31

// Self-service video honesty box on Nan's drive.

Movie Making

I'm not the type of person to sit around and wait for things to happen, well I have been, but not anymore. I was 43 this year for God's sake.

Just a few recuperative years after my wife left me for good, I decided not to mope around in others rejection any longer but instead avoid it completely. By that time, I had already set in motion my plan to become a world renowned actor but every rejection letter I received left me bedridden and back down to the bottom of a very deep hole of self-pity and internet abuse.

It was then that I started making my own films, initially re-editing old home movies to cut my wayward ex-wife's parts out, and then subsequently re-imagining key events from my days to immortalize onto VHS for future generations. In a rare moment of clarity amidst a decade of shite, I figured if no one was going to hand me a role in some Hollywood blockbuster willy-nilly, I would have to take my parts into my own hands and make my own vids. What's more, I realized I could do this all without ever leaving Bromsgrove, all from the comfort of my own (nan's) house.

With memories of my days at Blockbuster Video still fresh in mind, I began experimenting with a self-service video rental honesty box at the end of Nan's drive. I spent days making a custom built, on-site video rental cupboard where people could borrow my latest film and leave £1 in an ice cream tub for their troubles. Although I made no money via the project and fell victim to several petty thefts, I took the pillaging as all the encouragement needed to get out the rental game and push on with my filmmaking. This decision made safe in the knowledge that there was an appreciative audience out there in waiting. Of course, one cannot also ignore the impact of local pigeons getting into the cabinet and shitting all over the videos. Yet, I do still refuse to accept their actions as some sort of personal cinematic criticism.

For the past few years I have written, directed and acted in more than five hundred homemade feature films. Admittedly the first couple of hundred were a bit wobbly, before I got a tripod, but my acting has come on leaps and bounds since the introduction of Jessops level apparatus to my work. Happily, the prior experience of filming sans tripod has left me now capable of producing heart wrenching acting displays, whilst also holding up to four or five quite heavy objects out of shot.

After years of furious artistic graft, and living like a proper tramp in the process, I now find myself sitting on a potential cinematic gold mine. I have a body of work proven to have moved three generations of people (Nan, Mom and me) and reduced many of which to tears. I have to believe that break out success surely awaits.

What follows is a brief filmography of some of my comparatively better known movies, a mere taster selection culled from the mess of my current PC desktop. I am very aware that filmographies are usually organized by specific dates, and the same goes for my CV a few pages back. However, as I spend most my life trying to avoid such details I have chosen against including them here, save raking over old ground. Subject to some form of success, I do intend on making all my past work publicly available in a series of Tupac like retrospective releases. Ideally, I don't plan on having to die first to kick-start the whole thing though.

Filmography

Dermot O'Leary, The Life and Times of
One man production filmed on Samsung C3060R camera phone. Biopic. No Audio.

Ken Bruce Is Dead, Dead Air
One man production. Ken Bruce is brutally murdered by Dermot O'Leary in my mom's upstairs bathroom.

Pubes on a Balloon
Two man production. Real life story. Miscarriage of justice, thought provoking drama. Shot on Sony DCR-HC37 Handycam. Some digital interference.

Insects in the House
Documentary. Director, cameraman and voice-over artist.
Accompanied by music recorded off the radio. HD.

Nick Owen, Sleeping in the Red Lion Car Park
Street Performance. Played the part of a depressed Nick Owen
sleeping in a pub car park in Alvechurch. Cried real tears.
Reviewed well.

The Dolphin Centre Chute Remembered
Paddling pool recreation of the Dolphin Centre water chute in
Bromsgrove during its heyday in the nineties. Depicting major
players of the era and their subsequent demise into alcohol and
drug abuse. Two minute short.

Waiting for the Digital Clock on the Home Phone to Be 11.11 Again

Running time 48 hours. Prequel to the star-studded Uri Geller Biopic, *When I See the Number Eleven I Pray for Sick Children and World Peace*, featuring almost all of the cutlery drawer.

One Sad Man

Thirty second short that was borne out of leaving my camera running by mistake.

Waiting for the Washing Machine to Finish II

Remake of an old family home movie. My best and only functioning outfit in the world is in the wash, rendering me housebound, naked and cold until the cycle completes. Shot in Sony Handycam Anti-Panic-Attack mode.

Lilo on Dry Land

Homeward Bound style kid's adventure movie / heartbreaking allegory. 89 minutes. Shot using an HTC Magic phone, mixed ratio. Due to technical constraints, I could not upload the film, so the movie is exclusive to my phone handset.

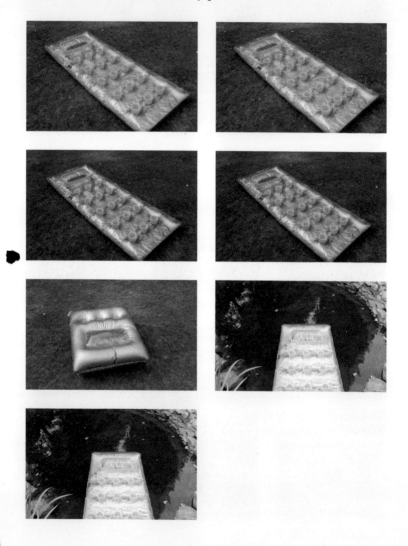

The Rise and Rise of Duncan Bannatyne OBE

This was written before Mr. Bannatyne's second divorce was made public and prior to him tweeting about killing himself. I filmed it retrospectively though, knowing what had happened but pretending I didn't, and I feel I dealt with the subject a lot more sombrely than I would have if I had shot it earlier. Lessons learnt all round.

Flat Lemonade or Day Old Water

Philosophical drama/game show pilot. Shot at my desk, in 100% solitude.

One Hundred Mile Prescription

A man commutes to Liverpool every time he needs a new prescription because his neighbour has started working in his local chemist and he doesn't want every bugger in town knowing his shit.

The Life of a Formula One Driver

Inspirational account of one man's rise to the top. Shot in and around Nan's bath tub.

Sullied Butter

An almost silent movie. Black and white video footage accompanied with only the slightest hum of the fridge and ticking of the kitchen clock. Bleak.

My Life's Achievements to Date

Thirty second short. Sad portrayal of a misfit / promotional vid / corrupted DVD.

Loft Lagging of the Star(r)s

~~I am told by a reliable source that I have the same loft lagging as Redditch resident Freddie Starr. This movie examines the persistence of loneliness even when you make it to the top and discover the material trappings of success.~~ Made prior to 2012 allegations. Encoded Secam video format / compatible for Uzbekistan, Tonga, Tahiti and Romania only.

Airing Cupboard Boiler of the Star(r)s

~~Sequel to *Loft Lagging of the Star(r)s*. Deals with the same issues of the loneliness of success and home improvement.~~

Plugs and Multi-Plugs

Atmospheric art piece driven by some truly stunning plugs.

I am Legend

Post-apocalyptic film shot in Bromsgrove. A man wonders if he is the last living human being left on earth after not speaking to or seeing any other person for a fortnight.

Martin Keown in the Shoe Cupboard

Filmed entirely on an empty stomach. I can't really remember what this one was about now to be honest. Shot over the same period as *I am Legend*, once again exclusively in the absence of human contact. A very dark hour of my life.

The Internet

The internet explained.

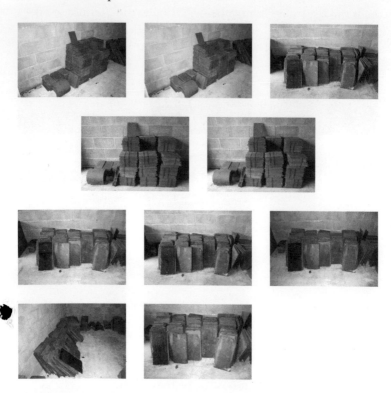

Dull Love

Hidden camera exposé of a very unhappy fun day out. Some footage used as evidence in divorce proceedings.

Shit Ladder

Upholstered Transformers

Paul McKenna Superstar
Half-finished NLP rock opera. A hole in the ceiling prompts a man to question everything he has ever learned. Fire alarm accompanied by lyrics from Paul McKenna's greatest hits.

Unboxing Regret
Removing wedding presents from original packaging complete with anecdotes and accusations.

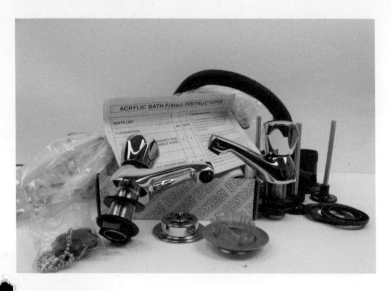

Dismal Weekend

  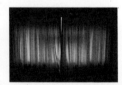

My Other Films

Shit Pillow

The Benefit of Hindsight

Ripped off for Six Years
by Audible.co.uk

Is There A Bromsgrove
in Heaven?

The eBay Dispute

Every Mistake I Have Ever
Made, Part Two

Fish Dead, Accept It

The Shed, Pat Nevin,
Why?

Lamentable Answer Phone
Messages 1–14

Wrong Doings Part One

Unfair Dismissal

The Main Differences
Between Me and David
Beckham OBE
(A Fully Itemised List)

The Wrong Number

VHS Prime

Pond Life

Human Sack

Rigid Hug

A Man Called Domonic

You've Been Diddled

Things I Might Have Said

Fat Mascot

The Ink Cartridge Return

Everything That Is Wrong
with the World
(Midlands Specific)

Bad Haircut

The Man in Tesco Express
and What He Bought

Jermain Defoe's Goals
Beyond Retirement

Long Term Gut

Don't Ever Go in That
Drawer Again

Direct Debit from Hell

Piers Morgan, The Day
of Judgement

Mufti Day The Movie

The Window Cleaner

Grown Up Love, The
Story of Gillian Taylforth

Highly Critical Lover

Car Crash Love Life

Depressing Burger

Bad Holiday

MSN Conversations
Between The Stars

Suspect Lump

Poundland Consequence

My Beloved Parcel Tape

The Heat Lump

Horrid Carpet

Ashley Blake, The Verdict

Goddamn Millennium

The Women Who Left

The External Hard Drive
of Sadness

Crusty Sugar

Tribal Tattoo Woman

Uncle Carbuncle

Dingleside Story

Secondhand Tracksuit

Bottom of the Food Chain,
Forty Years at the

Downright Wrong

Nothing Has Ever Just
Cropped Up

Teleshopping for a Further
Purpose

What Could Have Been	The Man Who Swallowed a Swimming Pool
Worsening Cereal Situation	
	Disciplinary and Grievance Procedures
Portakabin Memories	
Permanent Slump	New Toothbrush (How The Hell Have I Been Living Mom)
Yellowy Stain	
Dismal Fleece	Terminator Toupée
Dank Smell	Double Dip Regression
Long Term Grievance II	Hospitalized Relative
Car Boot Pervert	The Tupperware Complaint
Brass Hound	I Did a Few Strange Things on the High Street
Looking for a Lozenge	
	Don't Talk to Me About Public Speaking 14
Car Park II (Suicide Watch)	
Journeyman Hermit	Botched Op
Bogged Down in Bullshit	Categorical No
Physically Melancholic	Deflated Balance Ball Speaks Volumes
Unfortunate Growth Spurt, The Life of Macaulay Culkin	Limited Opportunity World

In Production

Bandwidth Bastard
Trevor only visits family and friends to download.

Barry You Smell Like a Bonfire
Barry smells like a bonfire. This film examines why.

**On the Brink with the England Fan's Brass Band
(The Hollow Horns of Misery)**
The England fan's brass band follow an innocent man around
playing the same songs to him all day every day until he eventually kills himself.

Eighty Percent is Good Enough for Me
A film about getting the right zoom length on the page in
Microsoft Word.

Photoshopped Sack of Shit
My ex-wife has photoshopped me out of all the existing photographs of the two of us and replaced them with images of an
actual sack of shit. It's a brown sack with 'Sack of Shit' written
on it and it's all over her Facebook. Anyway, what I'm saying
with this movie is Photoshop not only gives women issues but
also divorced men like me too.

Critical Reaction

Criticism, you cannot avoid it. Wherever you go, whatever you do, someone will hate you and want nothing more than to see you fall flat on your arse and go running home to your nan and mother crying.

We all know the drill, you tell people you are going to lose two stone by Christmas, you wind up putting one on and then they think that gives them the right to take your character to pieces. So you dust yourself off from that, read a few books, watch a few webinars and tell people you are going to sort your life out in time for the new year. Anyway, the seven day plan winds up taking decades and the results are somewhat less remarkable than imagined, and now somehow at every family party the jokes on you. Well no. No one's going to piss in my pants any longer because I have built myself a superhero shield.

Yes, that's right, I have upgraded the software for my mind to deflect criticism and make me stronger and better than ever. Now this process is still in its infant stages and I have had a few setbacks of late, but no critic is going to ruin my day, let alone my month, ever again. All going according to plan, by the time you read this I should have begun to notice an exponential change in my confidence levels, finances, career and the way people treat me. Picture me wealthy, famous and leading a glamorous lifestyle, laying on some all-inclusive sun lounger with free drinks. Now picture some catty remark in a local Bromsgrove paper whilst I am hundreds of thousands of miles away sunning myself, do you think that will bother me? No, I have found the owner's manual for my brain folks, I have taken the time out to learn how to work my own mind. Plus everyone at that local paper is an absolute prick, bar-none.

What these critics seem to forget is that, in many ways, they cannot touch me. Even before my new mental armour, there was nothing they could say to me that was any worse than what I was mentally saying to myself. To be honest some of it came as a welcome break. Certainly, there have been harsh remarks, but almost never without some form of silver lining, a concept internally foreign to me for many a year.

I am the master of my fate now, I choose exactly what to lay in bed worrying about, no one else. I will not be dragged back down to the bottom of an uphill cycle of bullshit by the mean gravitational pull of embittered local journalists. Sure, I might not legally be able to drive a real car, but I am driving my life and I'm driving it like Michael Schumacher with super powers. I have inverted all my natural instincts and now from every shit cloud I choose to only remember the fluffy bits. From this day forth any criticism I receive will merely be a passing murmur on the road to success. If not then the sheer weight of my own evaluations will pale all oncomers into mild insignificance.

Career High Point

My acting career has taken a while to truly, globally take off since I started in June 2009, mainly due to the fact that I spent the majority of the initial six months in bed. My career high point, however, comes from a street performance I did a few months back portraying a dishevelled Nick Owen sleeping in his car by the recycling bins in the Red Lion car park, Alvechurch. As I only hold a provisional driving license, my nan did have to accompany me for the full 24 hours which only added to the drama. The local paper said I caught the despair in Owen's eyes perfectly or something to that effect.

Recreation of the Nick Owen role, on Nan's driveway. //

53

A Lesson in Disappointment

ANY readers struggling with their self-esteem should go and see Wesley Henry in his latest 'performance', it will make you feel better about yourself.

As many of you will know Wesley has been writing letters to this paper every week for the past six months, literally begging me for a review of one of his films. However, before this week I had always managed to avoid such requests.

Alas, it was under somewhat false pretences that I was enticed out to the Bromsgrove 'filmmaker's' latest movie premiere. His agent, Mr. Jonny Sheaths, assuring me that two 'very big celebrities' would also be in attendance. (More on this later.)

Prior to the engagement, in a series of often bewildering text messages, sent from a variety of different phone numbers Mr. Sheaths instructed me to arrive at the venue (Wesley's nan's house) dressed for 'full red carpet treatment' but with swimming shorts on underneath ready for some 'red hot, hot tub action'. I was told to expect 'the biggest show Stoke Pound has ever seen.'

Sadly, all this never materialised, and it was only by the daubings on the wheelie bin outside the house that I realized I had the correct address. No signs of the 'once in a lifetime razzmatazz', no red carpet, no photographers; just an old sofa left out in the rain and a bust up wreck of a Rover200, a sign of things to come.

Upon entering the premiere (Wesley's nan's porch) I, along with two other men (I'm pretty sure they were homeless) was escorted up to a second floor bedroom by Wesley's nan. We then all sat perched on a single bed for 25 awkward minutes as an argument seemed to be fought behind a closed bathroom door down the hall.

Then just when all hope seemed lost we finally watched on in amazement as Wesley stumbled into his bedroom dressed only in bath towels asking us to 'Please not tell anybody about this'.

Mr. Henry, 43 of Stoke Pound, then went on to explain that his 'A-list' celebrities, Big Brother 6's Kinga and Rick Edwards (T4) had let him down at the last minute despite what his agent, Sheaths, had called 'stonewall negotiations on Twitter'.

The homeless men now snug under the bed sheets, Wesley began to read aloud a long list of complaints about the world he had just composed in the bath. Upon finishing the list, he then unexpectedly asked us all to leave as we were looking directly at him and it was putting him off.

It took Mr. Henry's mother (called home from work by Wesley's nan) to calm the situation, drawing the curtains and forcibly cajoling Henry into pressing play on his PC to start his new film, 'The Tupperware Complaint'.

The hour long film of uncut material ostensibly portrayed a disagreement about a piece of Tupperware bought by Henry in Droitwich, 1994. Nothing if not prolific, this is Wesley's fourth movie dealing with the encounter and comes off the back of another sixteen other projects completed last month.

Of the film in question very little can be said. If the intention of this film was to perfectly encapsulate the experience of disappointment, mind gnawing frustration and that feeling of wishing you were anywhere else in the world at the time of watching, then yes it was a success.

I have to admit come the movies conclusion there was not an open eye in the house, Henry's family included. I left the premiere ecstatic to get out the place, never as happy just to be me. Even the two homeless guys left with a new spring in their step, truly life affirming stuff.

// Review by Rod Johnson, The Hagley Times.

Reviews

Nick Owen, Sleeping in a Car Park
You cannot help but despair at Wesley Henry's performance. Hard to watch, hard to look away from, like a car crash happening live before your eyes with the inevitable emotional trauma left lingering for all involved. I have only the deepest sympathy for his poor nan.
The Bromsgrove Star

The best advert ... ever made [*for unfulfilled dreams left well alone*].
The Redditch Adviser

What the hell have we done to deserve this?
Catshill Community Newsletter

The Terminator Toupée
Wesley Henry plays the self-indulgent mommy's boy with true ease adding a new perspective to the common conception of Arnold Schwarzenegger's Terminator character.
Mr. Jonathan Sheaths, letter to Charford Chap's Mag

Wesley Henry's name will now sit forever at the forefront of the list of everything that is dismal about amateur filmmaking. A truly depressing performance.
Mrs. Henry, letter to Claudia Winkleman

A psychologist's wet dream no doubt ... I think it's rather far-fetched to believe that even so much as the title of this film was conceived before any filming took place.
The Church Hill Herald

A Surreal Encounter with a 'Tortured Genius'

AFTER weeks of anticipation I finally meet Stoke Pound resident Wesley Henry at Birmingham Coach Station, Digbeth. He is heading for the 'Big Smoke' and hopefully stardom at the London Actors Expo 2011.

This is my first encounter with Wesley Henry, tipped to be the 'future of Bromsgrove'. He was brought to my attention by his agent, Mr.Jonny Sheaths, who encouraged me to take this trip alongside Wesley today, as in his words it was a 'once in a lifetime opportunity for me to gain access to a star before he went global'.

It is 7.30am and Wesley looks tired and unkempt. My initial impression falls rather short of my expectations, but conscious of his reputation and prolific work rate, I am mindful I may well be meeting Wesley in character, of which I am informed he has many.

Boarding the coach Wesley declines the opportunity to have two seats to himself; instead he insists I 'scooch' up so he can sit next to me. He then puts his coat over his head and falls asleep. Wesley certainly is an unconventional character and gives off the strong aroma of a tortured genius.

An hour in to our trip Wesley suddenly awakes gasping 'I need the toilet'. However, the on-board facility is out of use. Increasingly agitated, Wesley shouts 'I really, really need the toilet now!' and gets me to go and tell the driver.

With a service station stop promised in thirty minutes Wesley's mood lightens slightly and he agrees to talk more about his latest project. Wesley hands me one of his headphone ear pieces and wedges his phone between the two seats in front before putting his coat over both our heads creating what he calls 'a cinema like experience'. He later tweets this to have been the world premiere of new film 'Lilo on Dry Land'.

From the corner of my eye I can see Wesley reciting every word throughout the film, at certain points he shakes the seat to increase the action and at one point he slaps me around the face. Though the movie premise can only be described as astonishingly simple, one has to admire Wesley's dedication to his art and the tremendous amount of strain and mental anguish he puts himself through making it.

As the film concludes I ask Wesley what motivates his projects, this sets forth a twenty minute vent about his ex-wife, cut short only when in one baffling moment he spills his drink all over his lap in what one might call suspicious circumstances.

In a slightly over dramatized manner Wesley had screamed 'Oh no!', before proceeding to tip half a bottle of Lucozade into his crotch. Yellow 'liquid' now trickling down the aisle the driver shortly pulls into the services, but Wesley now proclaims that he no longer needs the toilet. With everyone on the coach questioning whether Wesley had just pissed himself, he goes back under his coat. When I attempt to broach the subject I am advised to leave it well alone.

The remainder of the journey passes relatively trouble free and we arrive in London undeterred by the journey's mishap. Wesley is pleased to see it is raining outside. 'Just looks like I've been caught in the rain now, hey'.

Wesley has taken the unusual step of choosing to exhibit himself at the Expo by performing live in his own exhibition space with no set or promotional material. Show organiser Ben Pulmer stops by and whilst applauding Wesley's entrepreneurial spirit he also suggests that Wesley might have 'slightly missed the point.'

Passers-by seem to mistake Wesley's live dramatics for a stray member of the public performing acts of self-flagellation, and soon the St. Johns Ambulance arrive on the scene, very quickly followed by the venue security.

After an hour or so at the exhibition, Wesley says he is tired and complains of feeling 'London sticky'. He declares that he is going to McDonald's and then 'f***ing off back home'.

The coach journey home is a long and sombre one. Wesley seems locked in an inner dialogue, hidden beneath his coat again, occasionally muttering the odd 'what's the point?' or 'how many times?'. So it is with great surprise that I find Wesley in relatively buoyant mood as he finally pokes out from under his coat as we arrive back to Digbeth.

I ask the reason for Wesley's change of spirit. He informs me he has used the journey home to make a new picture filmed under his coat that he expects will 'blow quite a few people away'.

At the end of a strange day I feel I am no closer to discovering the intricacies behind the enigma that is Wesley Henry, but I am pleased to see him happy having made another movie out of the experience; the soon to be released 'National Express to London and Back (Same Old Dreams Gone Sour)'. Indeed.

//Article by Tom Don, The Finstall Eye.

Poundland Consequence

The first time I have ever seen a director appear five minutes into his own film, turn and talk directly into the camera and apologise to any viewers still watching. Bewildering.
The Oakenshaw Oracle

It is very difficult to establish light and shade in a drama when you have failed to remove the lens cap ... this kind of behaviour cannot go unnoticed for long.
Marlbrook Movie Forum

Bogged Down in Bullshit

One man's search for a song that will make him feel 100% better. However, don't expect a road movie, don't even expect any music. The search goes no further than Henry's bedroom desktop PC, with the final cherry on the filmmaking cake being the fact that all the music has been removed for copyright issues. Inspiration seldom seemed so absent.
Sidemoor Life

It is incredible to think how watching a man clicking through his iTunes library song by song in silence could ever be deemed worthy of a three-hour movie. Rewind it yourself.
Mark Park, self-service video rental honesty box customer

My Life's Work

Best bit was the buffering.
YouTube comment by jbagbigballs42

A big load of shit.
The Bromsgrove & Redditch Vindicator

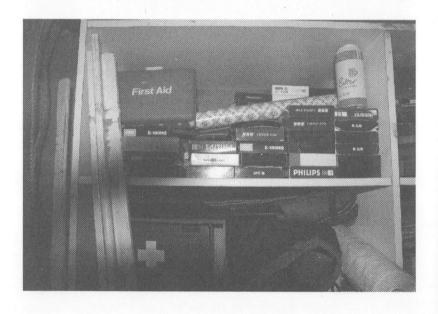

// *Still from Depressing Burger* (top). *VHS Prime* (bottom).

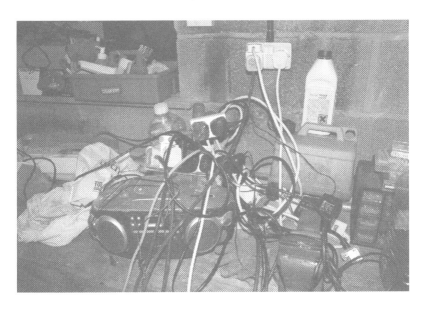

Bad Holiday (top). Plugs and Multi-Plugs (bottom). //   59

Wesley Henry Trivia

By Jonny Sheaths, Agent

After his wife left him, Wesley let himself slide to rack and ruin to such an extent that he cut off all contact with the outside world for four months. Unfortunately, no one noticed or cared. Wesley has since overseen half a decade of disasters whilst left to his own devices.

A lackadaisical approach to personal hygiene led Wesley, aged eight, to make his first ever film, *Me and My Antiseptic Cream*. The film inspired countless generations of bullies.

Wesley slept through the best years of his life and woke up one day with such an aching pain of regret that he tried to build a time machine. All this achieved, however, was to waste fourteen months more of his life and leave him addled with more guilt, self-loathing and debt.

Wesley shares his wardrobe with his nan.

Wesley's favourite song in the world is 'Slip Sliding Away' by Paul Simon. It was instrumental in him falling for his first wife Shelly as her middle name was Delores (the same name as the songs female protagonist). However, Shelly would later cheat on Wesley with both a Paul and a Simon.

Wesley prefers to advertise the array of truly 'odd' job services he provides under various pseudonyms in the local papers, as he doesn't want anyone in Bromsgrove, AKA his mom, knowing what he's up to.

Wesley still finds it hard to get out of bed most days.

//All these services are still available at the time of printing.

Ambitions

To be famous enough to reverse the effects of some of the lesser aspects of my personality and past. Get buff. Remarry, either Shelly or someone else. Cope.

Targets

I am a highly driven man, both in the sense that I need to be driven around a lot as I can't drive, and also because I am very determined. However, many of my targets seem to fluctuate depending on whatever TV programme I am watching at the time. To make sure you (the potential employer) and I (the potential talent) are singing off the same hymn sheet, I have taken the time to write down a few of my long term goals. Hopefully, together we can keep on track and tick every item off this list by the time of my 45th birthday.

- Jog with Obama.

- Put Sellotape on the back of the zapper to stop the batteries coming out.

- Put the mattress cover back over the mattress on my bed and take some pride in myself.

- Turn down a show on BBC Three.

- Make more water come out of the shower.

- Sort out the films in the downstairs toilet and turn them into a viable commercial entity.

- Slowly work my way across Graham Norton's sofa from the supporting star slot to the main guest seat.

- Try to get the birds in the garden to sit on my head and eat from my hands. Mostly the robins.

- Have some form of statue of me erected in Bromsgrove.

- Phone Dell and speak to Peter.

- Show my films at the Festival de Cannes, or Rubery Great Park Cinema.

- Put some decent clothes on.

- Win the acting equivalent of the men's 100 metre racein the Olympic Games.

- Secure a part on the daytime soap *Doctors* and then make the dream move over to *Hollyoaks*.

- Wipe the floor at the school reunion, this time strictly metaphorically.

Rider

In no way a deal breaker:

Haribo Sour Mix
Paul McKenna tape
Inflatable bed
Shoulder to cry on

How to Get in Touch

If you would like to get in touch to hire me as an actor, or any other kind of job, big or small, I am legally bound by contract to forward all interest to my agent:

Mr. Jonny Sheaths:
patrickpullman_872@rocketmail.com
0795 809 276 / 01527 5400 210

Jonny does tend to change his contact details quite regularly as, in his words, he likes to 'hide the cookie trail'. All this means that sometimes calls and emails can go unnoticed for months on end. For my own peace of mind, I would please request that I am copied in on all correspondence:

Wesley Henry:
djporky4@virginmedia.com
0770 2072 910 / 01527 802 260 (ask for Wesley)

Whilst you are there it would be even better still if you could also copy in my mom, ex-wife and nan to prove that all this hasn't been a complete waste of time and effort. Cheers.

Mom:
archers_fan23@freeserve.net.co.uk
01527 802 260 (ask for Mom)

Nan:
uksympathetic_lady@blueyonder.com

Ex-wife:
xxxshygirl69xxx@yahoo.com

2.

WRITING BY ME

Writing Portfolio

I am not only an actor but also a writer, odd job man and full-time emotional burden to my elderly nan and mother. All my creative output comes from the same place, all drenched in sadness, melancholy and Bromsgrove. In the coming section, I have selected a few pieces of my recent output for you to get a good look at the full breadth of my talent and mental frailties. Please note that what you see here is just the tip of the iceberg. There are thousands upon thousands more pages like these under my bed, up in the loft and filed in my GP's notes.

I work mainly in composing lists or short bullet point gists of ideas for things, so if people look over my shoulder on a bus they will think I am an organized man, not an emotional time bomb. Working with the right team around me, I am convinced these *gists* could turn into award winning movies / plays / television or radio shows / songs / poems / fine art / self-help schemes / toilet paper etc.

Occasionally in this book I have had a stab at expanding some of my ideas into more complex works. There are quite a few songs included which I do plan to eventually evolve into a musical of my life entitled *Wes Miserable*. However, on the whole I haven't got a clue what I'm meant to be doing.

As well as reading my emotional off-load, what better way to get to know my personal character than to have a nose through my Facebook and Twitter pages. You will find extracts from the last six months of each following this page, and then dispersed throughout the book. Let me warn you now, it does make quite harrowing reading.

// *Facebook entries slightly edited to remove requests to celebrities.*

<u>Wesley Henry's Facebook</u>

I woke up this morning
with no clean pants again
it's just really not how
things should be done.
10 June at 11:32

What the hell have I been
doing man?
10 June at 11:52

Just been crying on the
toilet.
10 June at 12:16

I've dribbled all down the
front of my cream chinos.
I just don't care anymore.
10 June at 12:24

It's such a low feeling
drying your crotch with
a hair dryer and the
neighbours seeing you.
10 June at 12:38

Smells like a dead wasp
on a 40 watt light bulb.
10 June at 12:40

I don't know where I'm going in life. I feel more

ashamed than I am burned.
It was the look on the
neighbour's kid's faces
that did it.
10 June at 13:21

Does anybody know how to
set up a Facebook account
under a famous person's
name? I can't seem to get
past the security quest-
ions. I've got no fight
left in me, I'm going back
to bed to watch a box set
in the dark.
10 June at 13:36

2003 was ten years ago,
I don't know how that
happened.
10 June at 13:54

I should never have gone
direct debit with Orange.
I'm so bloody stupid. My
magic number situation is
really just heartbreaking.
10 June at 14:01

I am eating dry plain
white bread folded over
on itself but it's been
in the freezer so it's not

how I wanted things to be
at all.
10 June at 14:33

What wife dumps her hus-
band the day he signs up
for a new mobile phone
tariff?
10 June at 14:46

I specifically asked her
that very morning if she
wanted to be my magic
number.
10 June at 14:52

I'm curled up in the foe-
tal position watching a
twelve part series in ten
minute instalments on
YouTube. I just feel numb.
10 June at 15:12

Such a waste.
10 June at 16:11

I'm having to watch an
episode in Dutch with
English subtitles whilst
using my left foot to
poke the mouse every now
and then so the screen
saver doesn't come up.

It is unbearable.
10 June at 16:38

Quite hungry now and it's
getting dark. I've been
in bed all day. Just can't
summon the strength to
put my sheets on properly.
I've got the box set blues.
10 June at 16:52

Spent the last few hours
waiting for the final episode to buffer but in the
end it was just one long
freeze frame and a link
to an Estonian porn site.
10 June at 17:11

Got no money in the bank
and the only person I can
talk to for free is off
somewhere getting boll-
ocked by a body builder
no doubt. This is the
exact opposite of success.
10 June at 17:26

Time creeps up on you so
slowly, the six o'clock
news used to be our dinner
time, I haven't even showered yet, it's probably too

late to bother now.
10 June at 18:16

At some point in my life
I am just going to have
to bite the bullet and
phone Orange.
10 June at 18:42

£40 a month is crippling
me both financially and
emotionally. There is
absolutely no sense in
having unlimited calls
and texts to a woman
who takes pleasure in
breaking my heart.
10 June at 18:58

I'm pretty sure she's
changed her number too.
10 June at 19:05

My stomach keeps on mak-
ing noises and the home
phone is ringing. Fucking
hell man.
10 June at 20:11

No matter how much I watch
on YouTube there is still
some other bullshit.
10 June at 22:25

It's really depressing
searching through a list
of the 100 best documen-
taries on the internet.
10 June at 23:36

If I am ever happy again
or if I ever make any
money I will never type
the words 'watch online
free' ever again.
11 June at 00:04

I can't watch anymore
films. In the last two
days I've fallen in love
with so many leading
ladies that I just feel
confused. My whole body
and mind feel wrenched
and torn.
11 June at 00:22

The more my downloaded
film collection grows the
more I just don't see the
point in showering.
11 June at 01:03

Was up last night watching
the best five films ever.
I feel like shit.
11 June at 11:43

Paul McKenna Self Hypnosis:
Supreme Self Confidence (Part 1)

Comments:

Has anyone got part two? I think I am
stuck in my deep sleep zone.
wesleyhenryhead

Come on guys, someone post the second
part I need this confidence ASAP. I
have to phone Orange about my phone
tariff. This is costing me money man.
wesleyhenryhead

Guys.
wesleyhenryhead

The List / Best List

Vicks Nasal Spray
Roll-on deodorant
Gaffer tape
Kettle filament
Paper napkins
Batteries

Winner! Winner! Chicken Dinner!

Winner! Winner! Chicken dinner!
Gambles at home on his PC
Wins big
Streams movies off the internet for free
In his garage / study
Redesigning Facebook from scratch
Covered his webcam with Blu-Tack
Has recently sold his car for scrap

How Are You Doing?

WH: Wesley Henry
BC: Bank Clerk

WH: I've got a scab on my arse, my collarbone and
my nose. I'm going to the bank.

[*At the bank.*]

BC: Yes, what do you want?

75

WH: I want to teach kids how to do something in front of TV cameras in an inner city comprehensive; maybe with learning difficulties, but definitely with problems at home.

BC: Okay, sounds good. How is your house price?

WH: It is falling down and I am strapped for cash because I have lost my job.

BC: Okay. See you later. Bye. Go away.

WH: Excuse me, before I go can I pick up some things from my security deposit box and can you stop kicking me under the table?

BC: What is it that you want?

WH: Please may I have the video tapes for the last ten years of our family holidays, I want to redub and reshoot the action.

BC: Do what you want it's your life, it's pathetic.

WH: Thank you. There are a pile of wasps on the hallway carpet I want to cut in to the videos.

BC: I don't care.

WH: Thank you. These tapes are all I have left.

BC: I've seen them tapes, they are shit. Now, please leave this instant. Get out of my sight.

Chicken Liver Parfait

Chicken liver parfait
In the sunshine
On the waste ground
Off a pen knife

Chicken liver parfait
In the moonlight
On the wet leaves
By the police tape

Chicken liver parfait
At the seaside
On the fair ride
In February or January

Chicken liver parfait
At the bus stop
On the roadside
By the car park of the scrap yard

Love

Person A: I love you darling.

Person B: Why?

Person A: It's something to do isn't it.

[*Extended period of silence.*]

Novelty Gift Idea (Posted to My Blog 4.1.11)

Someone the same age as you is far more successful
yearly wall chart / birthday card.

Nan's New Fella

Every inch the late night TV man
Artwork from IKEA
In his book an enigma
But in reality
A very sad scene
He sits refreshing the page
It does not change
He types like a whirlwind
'Qualified to satisfy you' reads his T-shirt
It is quite simply not true

The Presumptuous Psychiatrist

WH: Winston Henley
PP: Presumptuous Psychiatrist

PP: Would you like to tell me a little about why you
are here today?

WH: Erm, yeah well, the thing is…

PP: You have a very large unwieldy head?

WH: Well, kind of but…

PP: [*Ticking a box*] The women in your life think you are a joke?

WH: Well, maybe, but I've been...

PP: Crying yourself to sleep because of your baldness?

WH: No, not always the baldness, it's mainly...

PP: You still wet the bed because you hate yourself?

WH: No, not usually no, it's just everything in my life.

PP: Has been fucked up the wall?

WH: Erm...

PP: Because of your drinking?

WH: No, I don't drink...

PP: Is it drugs?

WH: No, I just want to...

PP: Kill yourself?

WH: No, well maybe sometimes, but I just want to find the reasons behind...

PP: Behind why no one respects you?

WH: No.

PP: Behind why no women will go near you?

WH: Well…

PP: You want to kill yourself because you are a waste of space?

WH: No, I just want to know why…

PP: Why you can't keep up an erection for more than five seconds?

WH: What?

PP: Why you cry every time you look in the mirror? Why even your own mother thinks you are a prick?

WH: [*Exasperated*] Why I can't get over my ex-wife leaving me for a brick shithouse!

PP: Ah, I was just about to say that [*stops a stopwatch*]. Okay, [*looks at notes for name*] Winston, what I am going to ask you to do now is lay back for me I am just going to put you into a meditative state.

WH: Did Mom really say that?

PP: Say what?

WH: The prick thing?

PP: Come on Winston it's your session today, now let's get this whale noises tape on til the hours up. Shhh.

Nervous People in Everyday Scenarios

A new show kind of like *Three Minute Wonders* on
Channel 4, but only thirty seconds long and focusing
purely on the complaints of a select group of indivi-
duals from Bromsgrove. Made in 3D.

Show One:
The checkout man at Matalan read my surname off my
bankcard and as I left said "Bye Mr. Henry" and this
startled me somewhat.

Show Two:
A message popped up to tell me I had a new email and
this did something odd to my stomach.

Show Three:
I put off going to the toilet for the whole of an eight
hour conference until it really hurt and I couldn't sit
still because it was nibbles and I had to smile a lot
(nibbles as in a buffet / finger food).

Other TV Programmes

Overdraft Exceeded Its Limit at Christmas, with
Davina Mccall.

Nasal Breathing Noises Confused with Women
Shouting the Name Steve, with Fern Cotton.

No One Can Afford Oasis Soft Drinks from Sports
Hall Vending Machines Anymore, with Rufus Hound.

I Have a Printer and You Can Print Things at My
House, with Jim Rosenthal.

Phone-ins That Changed the World, with DJ Spoony.

Everyone at the Business Start-up Programme Wants
a New Logo, with Joe Swash.

No Matter What You Say About Me, I Bet You Still
Want to See Me Naked and Would Have Sex with Me,
with Greg Rusedski and His Wife.

Fine Art Stuff (A Lifetime Retrospective)

Dettol in a Box File
VHS TV Compact on a Car Bonnet
IKEA Desk Lamp at the Ice Rink
Charity T-Shirt on a Bread Board
Watch Strap Inside a Plant Pot, Overturned
Hair Grip in a Toaster
Bird House Within a Haircut
Pillow in a Sink

Ex-Wife

Schnozzing about on Facebook
Looking for a change of relationship status.
A break up brightens up her day.

I haven't been on here for
a month because I have
been taking a long hard
look at myself. I've moved
up into the loft.
11 July at 12:06

  Wesley Henry to
  Jonny Sheaths:
Hi Jonny, I was just won-
dering whether you still
had my Slendertone that I
lent you on the 21st April
2009. I need it back now
because I am getting fit
for summer, specifically
the car boot season.

  We are a good way into
the season now and I do
ideally want to be taking
my top off at some point,
you never know what tal-
ent scouts are at these
things. Please don't let
me down.
12 July at 08:52

  JS to WH:
Hi pal, no chance it's
bloody long gone. I swap-
ped it for that bunch of

Quake CDR demo's I sent
your last showreel out on.
5MB of you, plus a 50MB
free Quake demo to fill
up the remaining disk
space, that was the deal,
remember? Still got some
left for a price if you're
going down the boots.
12 July at 09:35

  WH to JS:
What the hell were you
thinking? I gave you that
thing when I had every-
thing going for me and
now I have got nothing
and you have done me over.
I'm in tears here mate,
well done.
12 July at 09:44

  JS to WH:
Alright mate calm down,
the only reason you lent
it to me was because
Shelly found you putting
it on your lipstick.
12 July at 10:05

  WH to JS:
Well Shelly's gone now
isn't she Jon, like my old

Slendertone no doubt, off
with some nob-end with a
wallet and a six pack. I
really can't stand you at
the moment pal.
12 July at 10:46

JS to WH:
Please leave your attitude
in your bedroom in your
Mom's house Wesley Henry.
12 July at 11:50

WH to JS:
I know you only wanted it
because you heard it would
give you a five day permo.
12 July at 11:57

JS to WH:
Yeah well try this one
on for size, I didn't get
rid of it, I've had the
thing on permanently for
the last five years and
you ain't never getting
it back pal. I'm wearing
it now. Eve Pollard.
12 July at 13:34

WH to JS:
What are you on about?
12 July at 13:36

JS to WH:
She's coming to town this
Friday. And one of us is
going to have a definite
protrusion in his suit
trousers and it ain't you.
12 July at 13:42

WH to JS:
You're a dirty old home-
wrecker. I'll get fit
off my own back, get to
Hollywood and so help me
God never have anything
more to do with you.
12 July at 16:38

JS to WH:
Nice little speech Wesley.
Unfortunately you are
contracted to me for the
next twelve years.
12 July at 17:52

WH to JS:
That contract's not worth
the cereal packet it's
written on and you know
it. Every time I think
of my Slendertone I have
a pang. I never want to
speak to you again. Bye.
12 July at 18:12

ITV2 (Also Available on ITV2+1)

Martine McCutcheon adverts for yoghurts on ITV2
Seksy Wrist Wear by Sekonda on ITV2
Kerry Katona on holiday on ITV2
Death in the family on ITV2
Celebrities back gardens on ITV2
Shit on the doorstep on ITV2
Scum on the bath tub on ITV2
A man asks me if I am in the queue at Tesco Express
    and I say no on ITV2
An awkward silence at the Toby Carvery on ITV2
Kicked the ball over the fence and the dog popped it
    on ITV2
Slapped on the naked thigh on the backseat of a broke
    down coach on ITV2
Chips in a puddle of muck and piss on ITV2
Knock off pants and socks from your dodgy uncle
    on ITV2
A trapped finger in the car door on ITV2

Famous People That I Have Seen on Chatroulette

Premise for a chat show, inspired by real life, where I
click through thousands of strangers on Chatroullete
until I meet a famous person.

Pilot Episode: Click 6,583

Rocha John Rocha. I'm 90% certain it was him, because they had his face on big posters in Debenhams

when Mom took me to get a new outfit for uncle Paul's funeral. He was sat in front of a white painted breeze block wall and a shelving unit, holding paint cans, a toolbox and a broken torch.

He was talking about putting a 100 metre sprinter on to one of those fast moving flat escalator things they have at airports so they go even faster. He was looking for them to break a world record and then long jump off the end of it into a sandpit full of women. He's lost the plot. He was proper slagging off exercise bikes. He reckons the heart rate monitor thing is rigged on all of them.

He categorically told me there is no such thing as glass.

The Top Rated Film on Rotten Tomatoes / Best Ever Five Star Masterpiece

A film title solely aimed at mistaken Google search foot fall.

Factory Settings Betty (Forever Coming Soon)

A woman whose life story can be told via a series of static website holding pages.

Convinced there is a reset button hidden on her body somewhere Betty has spent days both arduous and pleasurable searching all about her person for said digit or dial, but alas to no avail.

Jam (Dialogue for a Film)

> **Woman:** Is that a tub of jam on your bed?
>
> **Man:** Yes, it is.
>
> **Woman:** Is it homemade?
>
> **Man:** Yes, it is just for dipping my finger in now and then.
>
> **Woman:** Are you diabetic?
>
> **Man:** No, just every time I sneeze I dip my finger in.
>
> **Woman:** Okay.
>
> **Man:** No, I'm not, no.

The Date

> Twelve year old romantic
> Third youngest of fourteen sons.
> Pomade, denim and a horrible loneliness.
> Waiting outside the cinema for the girl he left a note
>   for earlier.
> Scrawled in big blue matt emulsion letters across the
>   brown plywood door laying in the gravel below
>   her window;
> 'Meet me by the Odeon.'
> There was no space left to say what time or who it
>   was from.

// The Date. Past midnight at the Odeon, still waiting.

Pain Man (It's Written All Over His Face)

After years of constant sorrow, the word '*pain*' has literally etched itself into a man's forehead frown lines. Nobody will go near him. Then one day, upon catching a chance reflection of his face whilst being electrocuted, the man realises that if he really lifts his eyebrows and wrinkles his forehead he can make the word '*pain*' look like '*rain*'. He proceeds to go around town with a funny look on his face for the next ten years. It doesn't really solve his problems but he feels it's a move in the right direction.

Bob Watkins

[*Clearing out the stables away from prying eyes. Mint in gob, mop and bucket in hand. His coat is ridden with lint and horse hair. His face is all over the local paper. He won the spot the ball competition and was charged with attempted murder, all in the same week.*]

Voice from inside the stables: Bob pho–ooone!

Bob Watkins: Christ!

[*Walks across the tarmac to the phone in the pantry.*]

Bob Watkins: Okay, I'll take it down here.

[*Picks phone up.*]

Bob Watkins: Hello.

[*Person on phone speaks.*]

Bob Watkins: That's utter bullshit and you know it.

[*Person on phone speaks.*]

Bob Watkins: I tell you what then you can stuff your poxy spot the ball competition, but I'm getting my £250 pal.

[*Person on phone speaks.*]

Bob Watkins: Bullshit! I won that money fair and bloody square.

[*Person on phone speaks.*]

[*Bob Watkins smashes the phone off the receiver and slumps to the floor.*]

Bob Watkins: I'll get that £250.

Start of a blockbuster film. Bob Watkins battles to clear his name and get his £250 back. Court room drama uncovering conspiracy in the media, police and society as a whole.

Persistent Tiz / Sleeperman (TV Drama)

A man who cannot make any decision, large or small, without going to bed for two months to think about it first.

All Things To All Men / Derby (The Promised Land)

I have heard of a place called Derby
I know one day I will go there

I have heard of a place called Derby
Where the cool waters glide
And every soul is at peace

I have heard of a place called Derby
And one day, my darling, I shall find it

For I have heard of a place called Derby
A land of milk and honey
And all things to all men

Little Victories

Solitaire win percentage of 16%.
Establishing cover art for all songs in my iTunes
    library.
Making it past twenty / thirty / forty.

Me or Him

Him.

Morning guys, I just had a shave and washed my hair in the sink. I got my head stuck beneath the taps but it didn't hurt. I feel like a new man.
13 July at 09:47

Today was the first time in my life I have ever used the official Head & Shoulders two-in-one shampoo instead of the Tesco's one. The difference was negligible but just knowing I had the real deal made me feel great.
13 July at 9:53

I found a big vat of the stuff around the back of the closed down sports hall with half a Kettler cross trainer and a water damaged 36" BodyTrainer trampette.
13 July at 9:57

Had to wrestle some big pigeons for an old treadmill off the bonfire in the rear car park. I carried it back home on my head. Gonna set up a gym in the loft.
13 July at 10:07

I cross referenced everything with an old Argos catalogue in the loft and in 1989 I would've had about £200 worth of gym equipment. #FUJonnySheaths
13 July at 10:07

The treadmill belt was missing so I replaced it with Mom's old lino from the pantry. It goes okay but when it moves at speed the pattern on the lino starts strobing and makes you feel physically sick with all the bright shapes and colours.
13 July at 10:12

I looked at the belt for a split second and then I couldn't take my eyes off it. I think I briefly went into another dimension. I wound up slumped over a roof beam vomiting

inside a Fila holdall full
of my old school books.
3 July at 10:21

Finally finished retching.
The multi-gym is fitted.
Come up to my mom's loft
for a work out! Rooftop
views through the air
brick, basement prices,
just bring your own
torch and an inhaler.
4 July at 11:01

Had a fair bit of interest
in the loft space workout
arena, I think my life is
finally turning around.
I might get an ad out in
the paper.
4 July at 11:04

My mobile telephone just
rang for the first time
in fourteen months. It was
just Orange checking that
the number wasn't dormant.
But progress is progress.
14 July at 11:24

Slept like a baby. I've
been up since five comb-
ing my hair. I'm off into

town today to do a little
flyering for my new gym/
Support Your Local Movie
Star campaigns.
15 July at 09:10

Bit of a bad start. I just
fell over chasing the bus.
All that time spent doing
my hair was for nothing
it's all over the place
and when I try to rework
it the pomade stings the
grazes on my fingers. The
blood is literally gushing
out of me.
15 July at 09:18

Walking into town now.
Everybody's looking at me.
I am very conscious of
every muscle in my face.
I'm almost smiling, sort
of crying, limping and
sniffing all at once.
15 July at 09:21

Been hiding in the under-
pass licking my wounds.
I've fashioned a tourni-
quet out of the shopping
bag I had the flyers in.
15 July at 09:28

94

I've had to stuff the flyers down into the small groin pocket of my jeans as all the other pockets had sealed up with blood. This is getting on top of me now.
15 July at 09:32

Made it into town, a little bit sweaty and grazed from the walk. I think my eye balls are on fire.
15 July at 09:46

My pomade must have mixed with the sweat from my brow and run down into my eyes, setting forth a horrible chain of events which has resulted in me rubbing the grit from my grazed finger into my right retina. The pain is really something else.
15 July at 09:48

I am having trouble getting the flyers back out my small groin pocket with only one good arm. People keep on looking at me funny. Also, I think

a stray dog is following me. He keeps on trying to have sex with my leg.
15 July at 09:50

I went up and down the high street handing the flyers out but they were a little bit crumpled and bloody. People kept on telling me to 'F' off and then I got escorted out of Iceland.
15 July at 09:58

I tried that Leon off The Apprentice little finger trick to get people interested, but my finger was quite sticky from reworking the pomade in my hair and quite grazed from my fall. One woman looked visibly repulsed and then another older lady called me a deviant.
15 July at 10:02

Just got moved on from a bench I was sitting on. I'm really hitting a low now here.
15 July at 10:10

My old teacher must have seen me get escorted out of Iceland and off the bench. She came over and told me to sort my life out, before proceeding to steal my bus fare off the ground where I was laying.
15 July at 10:11

Some tramp just started a fight on me because he thought I had stolen his dog. I came to on the Kwik-Fit forecourt covered in something wet and smelly.
15 July at 13:48

Just got home to an empty house covered in blood and piss and then stood full weight on a carpet tack.
15 July at 14:34

I cannot believe what has happened here today. I can't stop shaking my head.
15 July at 14:44

Mom's gone away for the week so all I have to eat

is Harvest Crunch. I can't believe this is real life.
15 July at 14:48

Run out of Harvest Crunch now so going to have the last two Hob Nobs in a bowl with some milk for dinner. Christ.
15 July at 14:57

Just found a single sausage roll down the bottom of the freezer with about thirty odd peas. I am just constantly fighting back a tide of tears. I'm in a state of shock, I think I have been since about February, 2008.
15 July at 14:57

Little over an hour and forty minutes till Midlands Today, by all rights dinner should be at least be in preparation by now. I don't know where my next meal is coming from. I'm all alone, I feel like Nick Owen.
15 July at 16:53

Insects in the House (Film Trailer Script)

Up in the loft

Down on the landing

In the airing cupboard

Off the lean to

Beside the greenhouse

Beneath the porch light

Around the patio

On the front drive

By the fence

Behind the shed

In the wall lights

Amongst the golf clubs

In the garage

On the carpet

Insects in the house

Now in HD

Who is the Mystery Celebrity?

> Drinking water out of a glass that previously had milk
> in it.
> Back in bed in his work clothes.
> No dinner, no passers-by, just dust and long languid
> evenings streaming television from his laptop.
> He knows he needs the toilet but can't be bothered to
> get up to go.

Missed Opportunities / People Falling in Love Quietly (MOPFILQ)

> A new Saturday night dating programme kind of
> like *Blind Date* or *Take Me Out*. Contestants sit in
> a confined space, like a train or bus, and fall in love
> quietly without speaking and then never see each
> other ever again.

Alan Shearer's Hair Island (Widows Peak Elegy)

> Alan Shearer's island of hair is gone for good
> Security guard doesn't wave
> But he wanted to
> Car park pass fluorescent on the dash
> Motorway lights drift through memories back
> To the Premier League '96, number nine
> Only realised in the moment
> It was a different time
>
> All the videos suddenly seem old now

Nick Owen (No Autocue in Real Life)

Nick Owen stumbled over his words
God forgive him, he sleeps in his car tonight.
Bittersweet melancholy, 4 a.m. cricket on the radio.
Parked by the recycling bins;
It keeps the bonnet clear of the leaves.
He just killed a sheep and dragged it off to the
    roadside.
Scrolled through his phone book but there was
    nobody he could talk to on a weeknight.
He's feeling the cold in his legs
Pulled his blanket up over his head.

In the morning, there is a look in his eye
It would break your heart.

Local News Presenter

Run out of places to go with people he doesn't know.
Like a six time loser scratching out National Express
    bus routes in biro.
Sat there behind the glass passing by his old haunts in
    old clothes he wouldn't be seen dead in.
And in the dark of the depot there's no one left to look
    for, but he remembers a face from twenty years ago.
Down on the bench
His heart missed a beat
For the first time in a decade.

It wasn't her.

// *People Falling in Love Quietly in the Park. MOPFILQ spin off.*

The Whole Family Should Be Shot Dead...

But it is okay, because I am not talking about a real life
family, I am talking about a TV soap family all played
by poor actors.

Working at Home (Building an Empire or Digging a Hole)

Lack of productive days
Trying to pluck out nasal hair with thumb and
    forefinger
All I have done today is send three emails
I am overwhelmingly tired and stressed
Off my face on nervous energy
My body is a mess
Alone in any other room
Staring at the wall for a break
Working full-time at home just to get half a job done

I feel rank
My eyes have completely gone
You cannot get through this layer of sleep
I hate the internet but I cannot get off it
It's bloody useless
It's made me bloody useless
One more page open I swear I will collapse
Working full-time at home just to get half a job done

The man just wants to be cheered up
So he goes to the local service station for fun
You've seen his face on the forecourt before
No one wants to go round his for lunch

Worked forty years to afford towels he can't even touch
He had a wank
Had a bath
I hope to god I don't turn out like that
Working full-time at home just to get half a job done

I Feel Awful For

Calling the Police / growing up / Sunday morning /
the toilet / your dog / the mattress / misunderstanding
your lyrics / the blister / the gun battle / the burglary /
the baseball hat / Paris / Bewdly.

Depressed Second Hand Car Salesman Part One

CS: Car Salesman
OM: Other Man

[*Man walks into the car salesman's office.*]

OM: Hello.

CS: Hello, how can I help you?

OM: I'm interested in the Volvo.

CS: Okay, bear with me a moment, I'll just get the keys.

[*The salesman lets out a deep sigh and then gropes about a
bit on his messy desk.*]

CS: They're here somewhere…

[*Then his jacket pockets.*]

CS: Hold on.

[*Then his trouser pockets.*]

CS: Everything is all over the place since my wife left, sorry about this.

[*Salesman empties out a suitcase from under his desk.*]

CS: Excuse me a second.

[*Dumps a load of pants and socks on the desk.*]

CS: It's been a few months now.

[*Shakes out a sleeping bag.*]

CS: But I've still not found my feet.

[*Empties out a shopping bag from the bin.*]

CS: Just don't see the point anymore…

[*On hands and knees going through the contents of the bin on the floor.*]

CS: This business is on its arse. My son won't even return my calls.

[*Puts his hand into an old Pot Noodle pot.*]

CS: Country's gone to the dogs.

[*Empties a load of old WKD blue bottles onto carpet.*]

CS: Everything is just bullshit.

[*The keys fall out on the portakabin floor from inside a bunch of crumpled up tissues.*]

CS: Right then do you want to get in?

[*The salesman leads the way out to the Volvo trying to shake off a tissue that has attached itself to his trouser.*]

CS: It's actually one of the more comfortable cars to sleep in the Volvo.

[*Stares bleakly out onto the forecourt.*]

CS: Are you on Facebook?

Pop Stars and Their Problems

Polyester sweats
Meat sweats
National Express sweats
Perforated ear drum
Ingrown toenail
Mouth ulcer
Heat rash

Silent Fortnight (It Could Be Anything)

Go to Matchborough
Wait by the playing fields.

Store manager told his deputy
Go out and find me the laminator.

Until I die, this man's secrets I will keep.

Alone down by the old school wall
Late in the day.

Sees his old friends go by.
All the best to the lads.

One man turns to the other and says
'Don't feel bad'.

Sorry I Was Asleep

Yesterday / the day before that / last month / the past six
months / throughout 2011 / 2010 / 2009 / 2008 / 2007/
the past decade / the most recent millennium.

Just handing some busi-
ness cards out down the
tip. Some mornings I
really do wish I had a
direct line through to
Paul McKenna.
26 July at 10:00

Afternoon, I just got
beaten up.
30 July at 13:21

Aunt Sally burst into the
bogs and caught me trying
to pierce my left tit with
the kebab skewer she put
aside for the Sunday boot.
She went ballistic.
30 July at 13:24

My tits are in pieces
like. I just couldn't
face taking my top off
in Claire's Accessories
in front of everyone.
30 July at 13:26

Took a proper beating man.
There is blood everywhere,
I'm a 42 year old man and
I can't even pierce my own

tit properly. It really is
disappointing. Thank God
Mom is out the country.
30 July at 13:27

I'm in A&E now, Aunty Sal
says I need myself look-
ing at because she hadn't
cleaned the skewer since
Pete's 50th.
30 July at 13:31

The blood is weeping through my Hawaiian shirt.
The pain is really some-
thing else. This room is
so hot and everyone keeps
on whispering things.
30 July at 13:33

I keep on passing in and
out of consciousness and
the netting of my swim-
ming shorts is giving me
real problems on the pla-
stic chairs.
30 July at 13:36

I cannot believe what is
happening here. My uncle
Pete turned 60 three
bloody weeks ago.
30 July at 13:41

Been in bed all day thin-
king about what I have
done with my life. Found
it hard to concentrate
though because my left tit
is more chewed up than
the paper rim of a used
Calippo ice lolly.
31 July at 21:54

Was just playing with my
sore tit and I accident-
ally pushed the nipple in
and now it won't come back
out again. I am really
panicking now!
01 August at 23:45

I never really apprecia-
ted my tits until one was
hanging off me. I can't
breathe I think I'm dying.
01 August at 23:50

I just got bad feedback
on eBay I don't know how
much further down I can
go. I wish Mom was here.
02 September at 10:52

I think the roof may have
just fallen through.
02 September at 13:59

I say may, but I know it
has. I saw it happen.
It's all my fault.
02 September at 14:44

I fell through the loft
floor doing my weightlift-
ing a few weeks back but
I didn't tell Mom. I just
gaffer taped the hole up
and painted over it. Now
all my shit Christmases
have come at once.
02 September at 14:08

Not slept just paced up
and down the garden all
night. I've really gone
and done it this time.
#ReducedToTears
03 September at 11:14

Mom's back today. This
situation has grown in-
creasingly out of control.
I've left a post-it note
on the front door explain-
ing the house is now
uninhabitable. I am lay-
ing low, hiding in a bush.
43 in three days. Tits
like on off switches.
03 September at 15:58

If I Am Going Down I Am Going Down in Secret

Relocation TV show for people who are moving far away due to the current state of their lives.

Steve Ryder's House (Tear Jerker)

Voice-over: Steve Ryder is sitting in his lounge in his house coat. On a cold day, like today, there is nothing Steve likes more than a warm Ribena and some buttered Weetabix. However, if his wife is out, like today, then he just sits in the dark alone and waits for her to get back.

[*Forty minute fixed shot of Steve Ryder sat in the dark, accompanied by Annie Lennox's song 'Why' on loop.*]

Blockbuster Movie Pitch

[*A man walks into the bathroom singing, 'Banana, washed my grapes' to the tune of 'What's My Name' by Rihanna – only if we can get song clearance – if not he can just walk straight in not singing. The man proceeds to pull down his particulars and sit on the toilet. He then dials a number into his mobile phone.*]

[*On the phone.*]

Main man: Hello there, I had a missed call off you. What seems to be the problem?

[*Other person on phone speaks.*]

Main man: What's that noise?

[*Other person on phone speaks.*]

Main man: How about you ring me back when you've finished unloading the dishwasher?

[*Hangs up the phone, still sitting on the toilet.*]

Main man: [*Shaking his head.*] Amateur.

[*Plonk! Something in the toilet makes a splash.*]

Main man: Ah shit!

[*The main man gets up to wipe his bottom and realises he has urinated through the gap in the lid, it's orange. He tries to clean it up with toilet paper, but a puddle still remains on the floor. Now there is only one sheet of toilet paper left, so he uses that to clean himself up.*]

Main man: [*Solemnly ceases to wipe.*] Bloody hell man!

[*Our hero goes through his pockets and finds an old train ticket. He tries to soak up the remnants of the sad puddle with that, but it just floats. He thinks about mopping up the mess with his sock but then doesn't. The man then walks out slowly leaving the puddle behind in his wake.*]

[*To be shot in black and white. Starring Matt LeBlanc.*]

About a Dog

Person A: Oooh he likes you. [*About the dog.*]

Person B: He doesn't even care about me.

Feeling Low (Fictional Documentary Premise)

Alan Green is always depressed at the football, so why does he go? What are the real answers? I delved into the man's private life to get to the truth.

He gets paid.

He's too old to retrain and he hates being round the house even more so.

He also vomits into a used Bovril cup at half time and flings it down onto the crowd.

Wilson Hendrie (Retribution Flick)

Wilson Hendrie is a man who happened to fall into fashion once, by accident, for a two month spell in the late eighties. After being back out in the cold for a while now he has sensed the mood of the nation is turning back his way again. Everyone is penniless and worried now. What is hardship to them is just his average day-to-day life. At first he was happy to see others struggle down at his level, now he wants them off his patch.

Precious Memories (TV Couple Chit Chat)

Man: 2003 was a good year for us wasn't it?

Woman: What we were together then?

Man: Yes.

Woman: What properly?

Man: Yes.

Woman: Just casual like?

Man: No.

Woman: Mutually exclusive?

Man: Yes.

Woman: Hold on dear, I've just got to make a few phone calls. Don't go on the internet.

Mr.Jobless Guilt Man (Diary Extract / Superhero)

Things I have achieved today;

6.02 p.m. Waited till six o'clock for the guilt of doing nothing on a work day to pass.

7.00 p.m. Came up with an idea for a new superhero TV programme; *Mr. Jobless Guilt Man*. Basically the guy is your average superhero, but the twist is he only operates between nine to five and takes Sundays off.

Mr. Jobless Guilt Man doesn't have a day job, so is propelled by guilt to compensate by performing good deeds during normal office hours. However, come home time he likes to chill out just like everyone else. I can't quite work out what Mr. Jobless Guilt Man's super powers could be, but his catchphrase should be, *'Evenings and Sundays are for the jobless too'.*

Tsunami of Pop (Album Tracklisting)

1. Salmon en Croute (Taint' No Lie) (4:33)

2. Fidget in a MRI Scan (3:02)

3. Fake Pound (6:56)

4. The Clive's of this World (7:32)

5. It Gets Bigger When I Thump It (3:41)

6. You Wanna Get A Hanky Pal (5:51)

7. Tsunami of Pork (6:18)

8. Rundown Caravan (2:11)

9. Wet Handed Man (4:01)

10. Largely Ignored Person (15:12)

David Beckham

Inside the ramshackle pocket of his jacket worn
  through, sits a used chewing gum sandwiched
  between two old train tickets from journeys he
  never wished to go on.
He's sat down on a bench in Victoria Coach Station
  fashioning a shoe insole out of an old Tube map.
He's wearing headphones that are not plugged into
  anything.
He's got scabs on his chest that he's kept and main-
  tained for years for the joy of picking.
He spent his last 88p on a cheeseburger from
  McDonald's for breakfast.
It's 1 p.m. now and his Megabus doesn't leave till 5.30.
He just can't stop thinking about that chewing gum.

Live Chat Video Performer

The big bird with the dodgy teeth
Tracksuit jacket on, nothing underneath
Live stream from Sanders Park to Neath
Only logs on after dark, with sheath
She's a live chat video performer
Lives by me just round the corner
Too sick, too tired to do any damn thing other
Puts the kids to bed and she's ready so call her
Bending over on the DFS leather recliner
Kid's homework on the floor below her vagina
Her real names June but on here she's Regina
No one will touch her in town but she's big in China

Dear Google

My brain has stopped working and I find you partly responsible. I have no idea what I am doing. I wonder if my brain is full.

The M42 (Song for the Motorway)

Briar patch days
Painfully lucid nights
You look for reason
No one to talk to inside
The M42

The M42
From your bedroom window
You can hear it go
Takes the silence
Takes the road
The M42
Got in the car and left your mom
Rear view mirror shows your shadow moving on
The M42

The M42
Into the distance you can hear it roar
No one questions what you do
The M42
Singing at the wheel
Remembering the feeling you're leaving
Watching from your window
As the M42 goes by

A Life Time Blighted by What Society Deems as Trivial Afflictions (Pop Song)

I've had a slight headache since 2004
It keeps me from getting carried away with myself
It's not a joke
My life is not a joke

I remember all the bullshit you say
Then when you have left I take it up with your mom

You had a major serious illness
I have hay fever, mild asthma and allergies to animal
    fur and feather pillows
It's not a joke
My life is not a joke

I've had an on / off toothache since 2004
It keeps my feet on the ground
It's not the same
My pain is not the same as your pain
It does not quite wash with talent show judges

Doomed to wander forever on the fringes of society
With hay fever, mild asthma and allergies to animals
    and feather pillows.
It's not a joke

I want you to stop banging on about your holidays all
    the time

Paul Gambaccini will never make a phone call in
    my name

The Zoo (Kid's Story)

Peter went to the zoo today and saw many animals. He particularly liked the Snake House and feeding time at the Lion's Den. Elsewhere, there were elephants splashing in the water putting on a show. Unfortunately, Peter saw them being beaten when he went for a walk backstage. It was hugely upsetting and sadly he will now grow up a weirdo.

43rd Birthday Speech (Reference for Future Biopic)

Good afternoon, ladies and gentlemen, family and Mom's friends.

I have the undoubted honour of being the birthday boy today, and as such, I have the great pleasure of welcoming you all to the Bromsgrove Harvester for my 43rd birthday celebration. And what better place to celebrate my birthday than here in my birthplace of Bromsgrove, home to all my biggest failures and defeats. No, but really, it is great to see all of you who could make it here to share this day with me, and as for those who couldn't, well their absence speaks volumes.

[*Thank all guest(s) for gifts and well wishes.*]

Birthdays provide a great opportunity for family and friends to come together to celebrate a special occasion. Huddled here in this corner booth today, I would just like to thank you all for standing by me through these last few terrible years. Let's be honest, it's been a really awful millennium for me so far, and a darkness has seemed to loom over every move I have made.

[*Step forward proudly, space permitting.*]

[*Consider removing clothing.*]

Today, I stand here a portly 43 year old wreck of a man. Owner of a broken marriage, broken heart and a faulty fourth generation iPod. I look back often to birthdays gone by, before my wife abused my trust and prior to my shuffle function going to buggery and I am not too proud a man to admit I shed a tear. But, that is not why we have come together today; we are here to celebrate my making it to 43, and those of you who know me best know this is no mean achievement.

So, enjoy the meal. Enjoy the day. But, spare a thought for me, for I shall be going back to my normal life to-morrow. Back to a life of emptiness and pain where The Offspring's 'Pretty Fly (for a White Guy)' is the only song my iPod will play. Now, if I could ask you all to raise a glass to my mother, for having me and then taking me back in when Shelly threw me out to live with her current sack of shit.

To my mother.

I'm going to live at my nan's house with my mom because I made Mom's house uninhabitable.
03 September at 11:52

Back in my old close for the first time in twelve months and still the rumours show no sign of dying down.
03 September at 14:45

Buying a house two doors down from my nan seemed like a master stroke once, but now all those free chicken dinners have come home to roost.
03 September at 14:53

The feeling of failure is never quite so sharp as when you can hear your ex-wife having sex two doors down in a house you still partly own.
04 September at 00:23

It's nonstop. Every time you think it's stopped they start at it again.
04 September at 04:32

Had to get out. Just been drinking can after can of Red Bull sat opposite Blockbusters thinking of those pre-drop-off bin glory days. What a waste.
04 September at 16:23

I simply cannot believe I am 43 this week I had only just got used to being 42.
04 September at 16:40

For the past hour I've been searching celebrity birthday databases online and suddenly it all makes sense. Tim Henman, Kerry Katona, Greg Rusedski, Mathew Horne, Pat focking Nevin. All born on the same day as me. I never stood a bloody chance.
04 September at 19:51

I've been chucked on the slush pile guys it's a stitch up. I was finished from the get go.
04 September at 19:58

I'm drinking an orange juice, sitting alone in Wetherspoons, Bromsgrove. Everything is bullshit.
04 September at 17:48

My name's still all over the toilet walls thanks to my ex-wife's campaign to discredit me and gain a stranglehold on all our mutual friend's genitals. It's a bloody nightmare.
04 September at 19:44

Had to come home early, with a reputation like mine there is simply no way you can readjust yourself in public without Shelly's mates going on about it for months. The discomfort was almost biblical in its scale.
04 September at 18:12

I can hear Shelly at it again, she must know I'm back because she's opened all the windows and keeps on shouting 'BEST EVER, BEST EVER!'.
04 September at 22:12

Spent all day in the bath, just out the bath or thinking of having a bath. I can't stop crying, I look and feel like a pregnant lady in a birth pool.
05 September at 19:43

I've just got back from my birthday lunch at the Harvester. Attendance was affected somewhat by the weather and my past behaviour. #Disappointing
06 September at 14:58

I can see @MrJonnySheaths portakabin on the wasteground behind my nan's house. He keeps on poking the drains but he's meant to be getting me on the television.
06 September at 19:51

Seem to have my head in my hands in a lot of the birthday photos. I really just need to concentrate on getting myself fit for Christmas now.
09 September at 04:40

The beginning of the rest of my life in Nan's bath tub. //

(*Previous*) **Fully Clothed in the Bath**
Home DIY baptism/48-hour bath.

(*Right*) **Sat at the Bottom of the Stairs**
Collecting together all my remaining belongings from
my old house. Although I am wearing their 1995 away
shirt in this picture, I am not actually a Liverpool fan.
I just picked up the top as a memento on one of my
many prescription runs to the city.

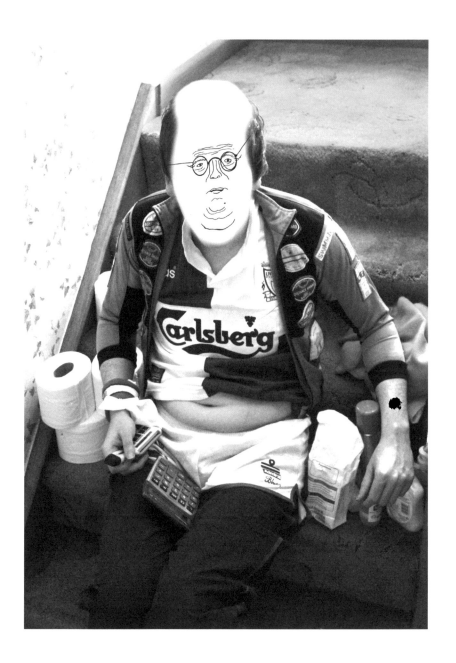

(*Right*) **Coming to Terms with the Present
(Shattered Dreams & Patio)**
Here I am standing on the remains of my old marital
home patio. The intention was to transport it slab by
slab from my old house to my nan's, but in the end
I just wound up smashing it to heck. You have to let
these things go, you can't hold onto the past.

(*Right*) **Back in the Bath**
Topping up the *'just been born'* feeling, following on from my DIY baptism.

(Left) **The Past is like a Foreign Country,**
My Ex-wife Sleeps with Waiters There
There is a lot to be said about moping, I get most of my
best film ideas and theories on what went wrong in the
past this way. But you have to learn where to draw the
line. Here I am sifting through all my old photographs,
ready to say goodbye and start afresh as part of a rather
messy spiritual re-birth. The whole process took over
sixteen hours including napping. In the end, the photographs only reiterated the fact that the first 43 years of
my life had been really quite shit.

(*Right*) **On the Scrapheap**
Mourning the death of my old shit life and
making way for a new one of international
superstardom. Shot at Jonny's scrapyard.

(*Next page*) **On the Scrapheap II**
I got the tracksuit I'm wearing in the photograph
when I was around twelve years old. I refound
it in the loft a few years back and it has been a
permanent fixture ever since. It is the one token
of my old life I have chosen to hold onto, the
airflow in that thing is fantastic.

(*Right*) **Setting Alight to the Past and All Its Grievances / Bullshit**
Posing for publicity shots by an unlit bonfire due to safety concerns surrounding the flammability of my shell suit. Nevertheless, the fire was soon to be ablaze and roared for several hours with the remnants of my past life and a fair whack of Nan's garden waste.

(*Left*) **Watering the Seeds of New Life**
On set at Nan's house, planting a potato and rebuilding my life. The T-shirt I am wearing was part of a two for £10 deal from Sports Direct. I got one T-shirt in blue and one in grey and they, along with a multipack of Donnay sport socks, acted as a catalyst for turning over a new leaf in my life.

(*Right*) **Slumped in the Toilet Cupboard**

In my dark hour of doubt and need, locked in the downstairs toilet cupboard. I let myself go here a bit, having come so far and yet again fallen prey to my old allergy to progress or success. I am quite a lonely man, I make no bones about it, but even for me this episode was a little excessive. I spent forty days and nights in that cupboard. Christ knows what I was thinking about.

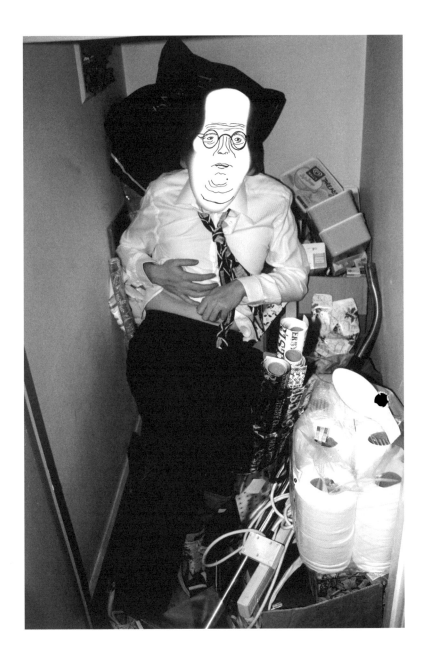

(*Above*) **Play Tent. Turning Pain into Movies**
I lived in this kid's play tent for the last few torrid weeks
of my marriage, watching on through the peephole as
Shelly settled Paul from LA Fitness into our marital home.
Needless to say, my head did get stuck in the peephole and
the proceeding trip to A&E with the pair was not one of
my finest hours. Here I am post rebirth filming a touching
tribute to that period of anguish.

(*Previous*) **Final Goodbyes/Skip Full of Crap**
Ten seconds after this photograph was taken I made the
call to the skip company for my old life to be collected.
Luckily enough, they didn't come for a few days so I
managed to salvage a few pairs of pants from the rubble
to tide me over until I well and truly hit the big time.

(*Right*) **Popped Signed Football from Julian Joachim**
Looking out onto the horizon and the future. Crying.

(*Above*) **Out in the Woods**
Bringing us right up to the present day with a still from
one of my current projects, '*Public Wet Patch II*'.

Bad Christmas. Too much online pool and self-abuse. Got to get back on top of things now. This is real life man. #FreshStart
06 January at 03:50

Woke up this morning to find the window cleaner has written swear words all over my window again.
04 September at 09:32

Nan said she wants me out the house during the day. Had to start working for Jonny again. It's not the best of starts to the new year but I've got to try to stay positive.
06 January at 10:38

Managed to fix my iPod, so I've been listening to Radiohead on loop with my coat over my head in the vacuum cupboard. Feels good to be back in the old work routine.
06 January at 11:02

I've just remembered that I hate this job and I hate Jonny also.
06 January at 11:29

No man should be patted on the head past the age of 32. 'Good boy' he says, 'good boy'. It's all just a bit demoralizing.
06 January at 11:34

Jonny just said I have to email him a screen grab every 30 minutes to prove I'm not looking for other jobs on his time. The guy's a stone wall prick.
06 January at 11:34

He keeps on having a go at me because he can hear me breathing.
06 January at 12:07

Looking back now I really regret all the time and energy I have wasted trying not to breathe.
06 January at 12:13

'I want this ironed', he says, 'anytime in the next

147

half hour darling'. He
treats me like a house-
wife from the 1940's.
06 January at 12:15

I said I would take him
to tribunal for harass-
ment in the workplace
but he said I should
be so lucky because he
ain't even paying me.
06 January at 12:18

I don't think anyone in
the local area under-
stands just what is going
on in this portakabin.
06 January at 12:58

The other day he called
me over to his desk just
to look at naked photo-
graphs of my ex-wife on
his phone. Then when he'd
finished he asked me in an
official capacity to text
her off my own phone telling her I still loved her.
06 January at 13:03

Set me back about twelve
years working at this
joint. I really hope this

isn't my prime.
06 January at 13:14

This can't be my prime.
06 January at 14:02

He's got me going through
the phone book telemar-
keting my relatives for
his new premium 24 hour
dial-a-condom hotline now.
I have to ask if they're
planning on having any
sex tonight and go through
the risks of unprotected
sex before letting them
know we do a condom drop-
off service- Dial-a-Jon.
It's really horrible.
06 January at 14:25

What the hell am I doing
here man? I don't think
I have ever even had a
prime. I don't remember
even a sniff of one.
06 January at 14:32

If I did have a prime, I'm
pretty sure comparatively
it would work out to have
been any other man's lull.
06 January at 14:36

Jonny just squirted half
a bottle of his 'Wash &
Go' at me, then bounced
the bottle off my head.
06 January at 14:43

He's printed 5000 leaflets
for the new campaign and
I noticed they all had
the wrong phone number
on them. It's all his own
bloody fault.
06 January at 14:45

I can't get my glasses
clean. I feel like I am
looking through a vac-
ant shop's whitewashed
windows. Still it's better
than watching Jonny wash
his balls in the sink.
06 January at 14:51

All the 'Wash & Go' from
my glasses has mixed
with the tears from my
eyes and now I am crying
a thick painful lather.
It's like when the kids
put washing up liquid in
a fountain but more sad.
This is definitely a lull.
06 January at 14:54

I've got to change the
phone number on all 5000
of them sex leaflets with
Tipex and a biro within
the next 45 minutes or
else Jonny said he will
start contacting random
numbers in my phone book
and inventing stories
about my private life.
06 January at 15:03

I haven't even got a blo-
ody private life.
06 January at 15:05

Just finished changing
the numbers but Jonny
doesn't like my writing.
He says my sevens look
like ones and my eights
look like smudges. He
wants me to start all
over again.
06 January at 15:52

If I saw all this happen-
ing on TV I wouldn't even
believe it man.
06 January at 16:58

Bloody starving, haven't
eaten all day. I think

Jonny took my packed lunch out my bag because it has vanished. There's just an empty Tupperware box and a post-it note saying 'I don't love you, from Mom' in his handwriting.
06 January at 17:04

He's talking to his mate Clarkey on the phone now, they're slagging me off on loud speaker as if I'm not even here, but I am here and they both know that.
06 January at 18:32

I just asked Jonny if I could go home soon and he told me to 'grow one'. Now he wants me to phone around getting quotes for putting a 'love-tub' into the office portakabin, it's past midnight.
07 January at 00:22

If this is my prime then I may as well pack up now.
07 January at 00:38

Just got another text from Jonny, from what I can make out he has told me to sleep here in the office portakabin tonight because he can't be arsed to come back to lock up. He's such a dickhead man.
07 January at 02:07

Not many people having the time of their life sleep in their boss's portakabin.
07 January at 02:46

When my movies hit the big time and I can fully support myself, I will definitely leave this job at some point.
07 January at 03:18

Give it six weeks and then I'll put my letter in.
07 January at 03:19

Leave once he has found a replacement, subject to opportunities.
07 January at 03:24

Work the odd weekend just to tide me over.
07 January at 03:34

Women (Song)

Grown man in cycling shorts
Uses catchphrases from TV adverts
In general conversation
What does he want?
He wants to start a family
What is holding him back?
Women

Oh women!
Oh women!

I just completed Tetris three times in a row
And I'm not even joking

Oh women!
Oh women!

Hanging off the words of a grown man in flip flops
Done nothing
Changed nothing
Made nothing
Said nothing
Learned nothing
Went to a festival last summer
And he still wears the wristband

Oh women!
Oh women!

I don't know why I am bothering telling you this
But Renault UK just emailed me

// Personal message to me from the window cleaner.

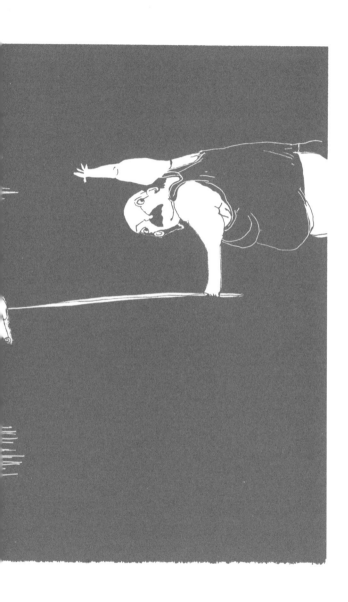

Interview with James May

WH: Do you ever clean your teeth in the shower?

JM: No.

WH: Do you ever shave your face in the shower?

JM: No.

WH: Nor me.

Gregg Wallace's Lonely Tuesday Evening Blues

Roaming the internet
Laptop in bed.
Bag of crisps for dinner.
Not washed today
Probably not going to tomorrow.

Places to Sit

1. Sit in front of a fire and look at it and you will feel good.

2. Sit in front of the sea and look at it and you will feel good.

3. Sit in front of a screen and look at it and you will feel awful.

Slogan to Live Your Life by for a Few Minutes (Flog on Some T-shirts or Something)

The distance between your bed and your desk is pro-
portionally relative to the level of your happiness.

The Lodger (Blocked Toilet Soul)

A heart grown cold and strange in the spare room
Tonight we pray for the lodger
Unknown and unwashed
And sleeping next door
Tonight we pray for the lodger
Will he ever get out of this decade long shit hole?

An empty space in the fridge of the last place he lived
Tonight we pray for the lodger
Nocturnal and still not washed yet
And just behind the other side of that door
Tonight we pray for the lodger
I'm telling you it's just one problem after another
    with that guy

Last night he dreamed of moving on
But today he's done fuck all
Tonight we pray for the lodger
Mind wrapped up in some other town
Plays his days in rewind
Tonight we pray for the lodger
An unpaid ferry boat man toiling between the same
    two shores forever more (his bed and his desk)
Tonight we pray for the lodger

Dear Tesco

After a brief chat with someone working in your Sou-
thcrest, Redditch store, on 12th October 2011, I have
taken it upon myself to make your new advertising
campaign. I believe the lad I spoke to was called Craig
or maybe Mike; he was something to do with the fruit
and veg bit. Anyway, he was quite keen to hear my
ideas, so please find the accompanying script and invoice attached. The advert has already been shot in my
house, but I will not deliver the VHS until payment is
received in full.

Yours sincerely,

Wesley Henry.

Biscuits (Idea for Tesco Advert)

Man: These biscuits are alright, where'd you get
these from?

Wife: Tesco.

[*Thirty minutes of silence.*]

Wife: Did you have the last biscuit?

Man: Yes.

Wife: I can't do this anymore.

Voice-over: Tesco. Every little helps.

Concept: Bleak drama played out through adverts like BT did, but with all the action purely shot in my house, re-enacting scenes from my failed marriage.

All parts played by Wesley Henry.

Invoice: £25,000

Characters featured in series:

Man: Down trodden pool of regret. Unappreciated for the genius he is.

Wife: The treacherous one. Less and less attractive as time passes by.

Life Coach: Like Enrique Iglesias but from Birmingham. Unbridled enthusiasm and a scarf on indoors. Untouched by life.

Last One at the Party (Autobiographical Ditty)

Last night a DJ shagged my wife
Last night a DJ shagged my wife
With a broken arm.

Last night a DJ shagged my wife
Last night a DJ shagged my wife
In a closed down sports hall.

Looking for Someone to Love or Even Just Slightly Get Along With

Conversation piece. Formally known as '*My Ex-Wife Let Me Down in the Megabowl Staff Toilets*'.

My ex-wife let me down in the Megabowl staff
    toilets. Six months later I asked her,
'Do you still love me honey?'
'I love you as much as I possibly can', she told me,
    'under the circumstances'.

Out of Work for the First Time in Thirty-five Years

Sourcing Christmas tree bulb replacements from
    Eastern European countries
Running international errands online for £4 items
I need a job
You had no right to fix my desk chair
I could have got a week's work out of that
All the door knobs have stopped squeaking
The locks are quite stiff, but at least I got them working
I need a task
The lads are ripping the front cover off the Radio
    Times for me to reattach
Wife's kicking doors off their hinges to keep me
    busy for a couple of hours
It snowed so I cleared the drive
Played solitaire
Sorted the files
But I need a job

I shifted thirty-five years backlog of crap out the loft
Put the stuff for eBay and charity in the right box
Started an inquest into my children's education
Sent the photographs to the relatives of their
    graduation
(They can't find a proper job either)
But I need a job
I wrote a letter of complaint to a daily paper
Found out the year shillings ceased to be legal tender
Chopped the wood and made a fire
Changed the bulbs and fixed the dryer
Mowed four types of stripe into what's left of the lawns
Repainted the walls, the floors and all the doors
I need a job

Back Home (Trance Anthem)

I think I slept off January
I had fourteen missed calls
But nothing worth mentioning.

Come on now
Get out of bed
Mom will be back from work soon.
Life is worth living
Sometimes.

Come on man.
It's probably not so serious.

Lost Her Weight But Also Her Tits

A timeless haircut and an evening of bullshit
The years pass by just staring back at herself
One half of a stable relationship built upon mutual
    regret, button up T-shirts and gout
Jean Whitlow is to hairdressing what Jackie Brambles
    is to slightly aging female daytime TV presenters
Solid and dependable, but nothing special
And this haunts her
She's enough on her plate
She's not just losing her weight
She's losing her tits

I am worried about the parking
But, for Christ's sake, who isn't?
All those men walking home alone pissing on
    car bonnets;
Aftershave on their boxers, just in case
They don't mind dying
It's just all the waiting around
Spent the weekend staring at the ground
Cos' Jean's not just slimming down
She's losing her tits

It's like listening to your old favourite band
And realising they are awful
Cos' Jean's not just lost her bellyful
She's lost her tits

Sleeping in the car in
the Foxlydiate car park.
Waiting for the Dial-a
Jon line to ring. This
is doing me no good.
18 January at 21:28

I have to be here as it's
the centralised perfect
place apparently. Right
next to the highway and
primed for dispatch,
except I haven't even
passed my driving test.
18 January at 21:33

Jonny said 'it doesn't
matter one jot because
it's night time' and that
it is all 'hypothetical'
anyway until I actually
receive a phone call.
18 January at 21:34

What's all this got to do
with my acting career?
18 January at 21:36

It's no wonder my life has
turned out like this, just
look at me. Sat in a car

park alone waiting for
phone calls off people who
want to have sex, it's no
way to live. Borderline
prostitution this is, but
without anybody actually
wanting me.
18 January at 21:39

Need the toilet. Need to
get married soon as well.
18 January at 21:46

I've got to be covering
40 odd square miles here.
On my tod in an Austin
Metro with the boot taped
down with gaffer tape.
It's just not how I envis-
aged my 40's. I don't
want to break the law.
18 January at 21:51

June from down the road's
son Mark is fifteen years
younger than me and he
has just bought a house.
18 January at 21:53

I'm a 43 year old man and
Jonny is marketing me like
a pizza boy. He just got
a Domino's Pizza delivery

leaflet and swapped the
word pizza for condom in
every occurrence.
18 January at 21:55

I'm sat here in a car park
on the off chance someone
might phone up wanting a
condom immediately in a
rural area.
18 January at 21:57

There's no way I can keep
up the '30 minute or Free'
guarantee, I can't even
drive man. If I do get
a call I'm going to have
to get Mom to drive over
here and give me a lift.
18 January at 21:58

No one is going to write a
film about this. It's just
pathetic.
18 January at 22:03

I know with Mom driving
the job I'm doing isn't
at all illegal but it
ain't gonna have much
clout with the extended
relatives come Christmas.
18 January at 22:06

'Not too dissimilar from
NHS organ driver job',
that's how I explained
it to Nan but that's not
going to wash with the
more pernickety ones.
18 January at 22:07

24 hour emergency condom
delivery makes no sense.
18 January at 22:09

Sleeping in a car makes
no sense.
18 January at 22:11

My head was not built to
cram under a mini metro
ceiling at 45°, it was
built for television,
national television.
18 January at 22:13

This is not a good situ-
ation to sit assessing
my life. It's colder in
the car than it is in
the outside.
18 January at 22:18

The car windows have all
steamed up to reveal hid-
den abuse Jonny must have

secretly written sometime last week. Right now the condensation above my head reads, 'This man shoves carrots up his arse'.
18 January at 22:24

Dear God what has real life come to? I could really do with going to the toilet now.
18 January at 22:29

It's nearly closing time, I'm supposed to be selling jonnies out the boot but it's too cold.
18 January at 22:38

I'm curled up in the passenger seat footwell with my coat over me again. I am in no state to face the general public.
18 January at 22:46

All I want is to be happy and I will sit here alone until that happens.
18 January at 22:48

Really need the goddamn toilet now but don't want

to go inside in case I see anyone I used to go to school with.
18 January at 22:51

Parts of my body feel like they may well explode and others feel like they may fall off. You really have to wonder what part God is playing in all this.
18 January at 22:59

Not allowed the heater or radio on as the battery has been on the blink since Jonny attached it to his tits last week.
18 January at 23:03

I think I need to go to confession.
18 January at 23:16

Just had to do a wee into a condom.
18 January at 23:19

It's steaming, leaking everywhere. I'd be lying if I said the warmth wasn't appreciated.
18 January at 23:21

Pin hole sized holes spur-
ting piss out the jonny
like a shower head.
18 January at 23:23

This product is totally
unfit for market. It's
full of holes. What kind
of show are we running
here? I need answers.
18 January at 23:27

Phoning Jonny this ain't
on. No way man, no way,
this is going to affect
real lives, I don't want
to be part of it no more,
I'm out. I'm out.
18 January at 23:29

Jonny says that the holes
are for added sensation
and that sperm can't go
through in any case as
it's thick. It makes sense
but nothing I've read on
the internet seems to
back that up.
18 January at 23:36

Piss balloon bigger than
my head between my legs.
18 January at 23:38

I think someone's looking
in the window.
18 January at 23:45

Got my own piss on my own
face. Oh Jesus why do I do
this to myself?
18 January at 23:50

There are people looking
in. I can't seem to get my
head to shrink.
18 January at 23:53

They think there's some-
thing valuable under the
coat I am hiding under
but it is just me.
18 January at 23:59

Every time I open my
mouth to breathe I get
a gobful of my own warm
piss. It's unforgiving.
Really quite base.
19 January at 00:07

I shouldn't be hiding in
a foot well at this stage
in my life. This is not
going to end well, I just
know it.
19 January at 00:31

The Almighty (Scripted Reality TV Show)

OS: Office Secretary
HP: Higher Power / GP

HP: What's the point?

OS: Because you have to.

HP: I don't give a shit.

OS: There are people out there waiting to see you.

HP: I don't give a shit about them, Sandra. Tell them
    I got sick.

OS: But you're not sick.

HP: They don't know that do they?

OS: But they saw you come in.

HP: Fuck off did they?!

OS: They did! There were four people at the door.

HP: For fuck's sake man.

OS: You can't keep them waiting all day.

HP: I don't need this shit, Sandra, just get rid of them.

OS: I've told them you will see them now.

HP: You haven't got a clue have you? You haven't got a fucking clue.

OS: Take your jacket off your head now, come on.

HP: Everything falls on me round here doesn't it?

OS: Pop your trousers back on now, Mr. Jones is coming in to see you now.

HP: What's the bloody point?

Physically Sick (Song / TV Show About the Physically Sick)

Physically sick, physically sick, physically sick
Everyone I ever met gets
Physically sick, physically sick, physically sick
From time to time
In my presence
Coincidences will occur

All Things Added Up (Advert Jingle)

All things added up
I'm going back to bed
All things added up
I'll be wearing the same clothes for weeks
All things added up
I'll call you to tell you to ring me back
All things added up
The possibility of a future holiday seems distant

Problems at Work (Film Dialogue)

Boss: Did you go to the toilet in my portakabin?

Employee: Yes.

Boss: You need to go to the doctor's pal.

Voicemail (Hero's Lament)

It's nearly four in the morning,
I can't get to sleep.
I think I've twisted my left testicle.
I won't be able to do my driving lesson tomorrow.
It's pretty bad this time.
This feels serious.
Please don't charge me.
I know it's not 24-hours' notice but just please don't
    charge me or at least do it pro-rata.
I'm giving you 15-hours' notice.
If you are still going to insist on charging me then
    just pick me up as normal.
I will make you wish you had waved the cancellation
    fee, that I promise.
Night night or good morning and just so you know it's
    3.45 a.m. now so that's actually over 15-hours'
    notice ... it is in no way my problem if you don't
    pick up your messages for another few hours.
I have informed you at 3.45 a.m.

It's starting to feel a bit better now.
See you tomorrow Dave.

The Real World Has Always Been a Problem (Hymn/Musical Complaint)

A lifetime avoiding the subject
A twenty-five year marriage out of politeness
A five year plan heavily reliant on scratchcards

It's depressing looking for a new house
When you have a perfectly good one already
It's depressing looking for a new life
When you have a perfectly good one already

What's life become?
Ex-wife's new boyfriend inviting me round for dinner
    at my own house
I really wish I hadn't gone

I took a photo to the barbers
I said I want what he's got
My old bed, shed and house, but;
The real world has always been a problem

What's it going to take to get some good memories?
I bought these trousers for a wedding
Now I wear them for days on end round the house

Weeping on an estate agent's shoulder
Whilst his mate steals the hubcaps off ya' nan's Rover
Weeping on an estate agent's shoulder
The last bastion of the sick and the lonely

Charity collectors walk up to me in the street and
    ask me what's gone wrong?

Ex-wife's new boyfriend inviting me round to dinner
    just to clean my own house
I really wish I hadn't gone

Up in the loft, praying to God
Sifting through what's left of life's meaning
In a perfectly decent pair of trousers with only one
    tiny rip at the bollock;
The real world has always been a problem

Shelly's New Chap (Trilogy of Clowns)

Failed MOT
Plasters on his fingers
Arm in a sling
Driving a digger
He changes dials from the passenger seat of any car
    he is in
Makes his own tea and gravy no matter whose house
    he is in
Saves his lemonade for special occasions
All those mornings you will never see again
Because he is watching MTV Base

Shelly's Ex-New Chap

The width of a wardrobe.
Always one to draw a crowd.
Applied to be on *Coach Trip, The X-Factor, Come Dine
    with Me* and *Britain's Got Talent.*
Appeared on the news; a practicing bigamist.

DVLA Test Centre Haircut Confusion

It's just bad timing, bad luck and a bad ponytail
It's just bad timing, bad luck and a bad ponytail

Too much time planning proposals to passing
strangers
Too many missed opportunities to pull out
Take me back to the test centre
I will sit in the back
Positioned on the left of the three back seats of the
vehicle, as to avoid my reflection in the rear-view
mirror, as I am really quite upset with myself

I hope you understand
It's just bad timing, bad luck and a bad ponytail
It's just bad timing, bad luck and a bad ponytail

Fan Club Badges (Merchandise Slogans)

Rethinking My Life Choices
Waiting for a Remarkable Turnaround for the Past
Decade or So
Slept Through the Best Years of My Life
All I Want to Do Today Is Have a Bath
Mom!!! Mom!!! I Got a Blow Job!!

Possible Character

A woman that can only answer '*get fucked*' to any
question ever asked.

Possible Character II

A man who misunderstands the word '*boring*' for the shopping destination *The Bullring, Birmingham*, whenever mentioned in conversation.

Cold

Man: It's cold isn't it?

Wife: No.

Man: I think it is.

Wife: I don't.

Man: I'm really cold.

Wife: I'm not.

Man: It's bloody freezing in here.

Wife: It isn't.

Statement of Intent (Life Plan)

Wake up.
Try not to feel tired.
Find something to do with the day.

(Stay off The Sun website.)

All I Want to Do Today Is Have a Bath

Watched the news on TV all day
Took a test on the internet for potential illnesses
    all night

Czechoslovakia!
Czechoslovakia!
STOKE

I've got a big old black dog
And it shits all over the place
All I want to do today is have a bath

Eight bags of dog's mess on the drive for Christmas
Nothing better than a cheapo vicar stalking around
    hospital corridors finishing uneaten suppers and
    watching *Emmerdale* on bedside televisions for free

Czechoslovakia!
Czechoslovakia!
STOKE

I am sorry to say the world of fashion has passed me by
All I want to do today is have a bath

Hot tap dunt work pal
Hot tap dunt work mate
Better go back and sit on the toilet for a bit

So far from the big fuck off Hollywood motor home
    we dreamt about;
It is disheartening, bathing in the afternoon

Here's a Sneak Preview of Something I Have Been Working On: (Promotional Tweet)

My self-esteem.

Here's Another Sneak Preview of Something I Have Been Working On:

My personal hygiene.

Start to a Radio Drama

Hello there,

My son recently got beaten up in your car park after falling foul of a couple of your regulars. I have no qualms about it, very few people like to get another person's piss on them. Wesley now agrees he deserved it, however, it was an honest mistake on his part, purely bladder related and nothing remotely sexual. That said I can see how the misunderstanding arose. Accidents will happen. Boys will be boys.

Anyway, the problem that Wesley faces now is, along with giving him a tasty little going over, the chaps in question also took a big blue IKEA bag of prophylactics that he was supposed to be selling in your car park that night. Obviously, any dispute you may have regarding the floundering of trading laws should be taken up with Wesley's boss, Mr. Jonny Sheaths. The difficulty is that Mr. Sheaths is now calling my son a petty thief and demanding quite a hefty sum of financial recompense, payable post-haste.

As I said, Mr. Sheaths doesn't believe the merchandise was stolen and is quite adamant in his belief that Wesley pocketed the money, or wasted all the condoms practising putting them on himself. These accusations are obviously unfounded and based on little more than local gossip stemming from a particularly low period in Wesley's post-divorce meltdown.

I'm hoping you will be able to clear my son's name by showing his boss your CCTV footage from the 19th January just after closing time.

I would also like to request that any video of the event should remain off the internet and that the blue IKEA bag is returned, as it was mine and holds a certain amount of sentimental value.

Please send my apologies to the men who beat Wesley up and tell them they are welcome to visit our house for tea any time they like.

Yours sincerely,

Mrs. Henry

Wesley Henry's Facebook

Jonny found an old condom machine on eBay for 99p and I have to pick it up because he said it will be a life lesson.
12 February at 08:48

The machine is in Woking. I am in Bromsgrove and I can't drive, still Jonny told me he doesn't give a shit.
12 February at 08:51

116 miles, two hours and six minute drive away. I think I might have to hitchhike, I can't face using the coaches.
12 February at 08:57

Just rang Mom, she said she will take the day off work to drive me but she's fucking furious.
12 February at 09:03

Going to try to make a day of it, really enjoy ourselves, bond.
12 February at 09:06

Mom's not talking to me.
12 February at 09:24

So many different feelings in my tummy it's hard to know what is what. I feel quite sick, guilty and nervous all at the same time. Ken Bruce isn't helping matters.
12 February at 09:48

Mom's driving like a maniac.
12 February at 10:23

The car's all over the road having to grab onto the roof handle. She's still not saying anything to me, lots of swearing at other cars though.
12 February at 10:27

Journey wasn't too bad apart from some mild travel sickness, treated myself to large Big Mac meal whilst Mom was in the toilet at the ser-vice station. Please don't tell her.
12 February at 11:48

Good to be out the office.
Definitely the best day
I've had this year.
12 February at 11:57

Had a bit of trouble finding a parking space and
Mom started bringing up
the past again. Going
to the pub to get the
machine now. Feel quite
nervous about it.
12 February at 12:03

I've got it!!! Doesn't look
quite as good as it did
in the photograph and it's
really dusty but can't
complain for 99p. I just
wanted to get out the
place to be honest.
12 February at 12:47

It's bloody heavy man,
probably should've asked
Mom to bring the car
round but I don't think
she would've been in
the mood.
12 February at 12:53

I'm perched on a wet bench
outside the pub avoiding

eye contact. I think I'm
going to need help with
this piece of shit but I
can't go back in to ask.
12 February at 12:54

The atmosphere in that
place felt like it could
quite quickly change
from that of a normal
business transaction to
one where I was taking
quite a solid beating.
12 February at 12:59

The landlord seemed angry
at me for Jonny getting
a 99p bargain. Plus he
looked at me funny when
I asked for the 1p change.
12 February at 13:03

Don't want to go back in
to that pub. I won't.
12 February at 13:04

I can't get Mom involved
either.
12 February at 13:07

I can't go running back to
Mommy every five minutes.
Those were her exact words

earlier. I have to do this
by myself. I can do this.
I have to do this.
12 February at 13:12

I said I could manage.
I said I could manage.
12 February at 13:13

Keeled over balancing the
machine on a bollard. Too
late to ring Mom now, the
place is pedestrianized.
I don't know how much
further I can carry this
weight, my hands are
giving up on me.
12 February at 13:22

This really is heavy. I'm
serious now. I've stopped
at every bench since the
pub. The sweat is pouring
off me, passers-by keep on
making comments.
12 February at 13:27

This is the hardest thing
I have ever done in my
entire life. I should not
have had that Big Mac
meal for lunch.
12 February at 13:33

This is heavier than a
person. I hate McDonalds.
12 February at 13:34

Feel sick. Every time I
put my leg down it wobbles
and I can no longer feel
my fingers.
12 February at 13:41

It's pinching my skin,
it's really pinching.
12 February at 13:43

Fucking hell man.
12 February at 13:45

I've got thick dust all
over my trousers, these
are only supposed to be
for Sunday best. They're
dry clean only. Mom's
going to go ballistic.
12 February at 13:48

I am feeling very, very
dizzy now.
12 February at 13:56

My eyeballs feel red hot.
Feel like I've been jog-
ging in a microwave.
12 February at 13:59

I think I have pulled a
hammy in my face.
12 February at 14:01

Done this too many times.
43 years old now, it's
just pathetic.
12 February at 14:04

I have definitely ripped
my trousers somehow. I
can feel the cold air on
my buttocks. Got to get
to the car now. It's not
the way to do things this.
12 February at 14:06

My mind is all over the
place, I can't stop beat-
ing myself up and then
apologising to myself,
it's like bloody ping
pong in here.
12 February at 14:09

What the hell am I doing
in Woking?
12 February at 14:12

Just caught my reflection.
Fucking hell. Not good,
not good.
12 February at 14:14

There is a large group of
bigger boys and they are
throwing things at me.
They are aiming stuff at
the hole in my trousers.
I think they have devised
a point system.
12 February at 14:19

A man just shouted 'nut
job' right at me as if I
wasn't aware of my situa-
tion. Like he was shouting
at a TV but I'm a real
life person.
12 February at 14:24

Why did I smile at him?
What's wrong with me?
12 February at 14:25

I have a blood blister on
my finger. I can do this.
12 February at 14:32

This is crazy, this
goddamn machine is
heavier than anything I
have ever lifted in my
entire life.
12 February at 14:37

To be continued...

Hope v Despair (A Philosophical Total Wipe Out)

Find two men, one with the name '*hope*' (Bob Hope for example) the other with the name '*despair*' (a Mr. Des Pear lives three doors down from me). Get them to compete against each other in a number of one on one activities. Then add the scores up to see whether *hope* conquers *despair*. If successful, the same could be done with a Mr. Triumph and Mr. Ad Versity, or Mr. Nature and Mr. Nurture. Dave Berry could present.

I Ate a Yoghurt (Plot Sequence)

I ate a yoghurt in such a fashion my mother
   disowned me.
I ate a yoghurt in a manner which lost me my home.
I ate a yoghurt just me and my loneliness.
I ate a yoghurt and made everything worse.

Low Ebb (Gist of a Play)

Just went to Asda and all I bought was one chicken drumstick from the deli counter.

He Wet Himself (Jovial Aside at a Funeral)

He wet himself crying.
He wet himself drinking.
He wet himself leaving.
But he never even laughed once.

// Hope v Despair. Senior Volleyball Match. One on One.

Good Night / The Story of a Marriage

Man: Good night darling, I love you.
Wife: Good night mate, I can just about bear you.

Man: Good night darling, I love you.
Wife: Just keep it down a bit would you.

Man: Good night darling, I love you.
Wife: Please don't contact me ever again.

Unforgivable Service at PC World

I'm not a bad man
I try to live a good life
But sometimes I'm pushed too far

Unforgivable service at PC World [x2]

And it just so happens we are related? Bullshit!
And so it just so happens you refuse to recognise my
    existence? Bullshit!
Anybody can read off an in-store display

I got the high blood pressure without the high paid
    job to cover it
The lads at the tip kicked the shit out my self-esteem
I got two buses just to get here and now you're push-
    ing me just that bit too far upstream

Unforgivable service at PC World [x2]
And, by the way, Shane your front lawn is a disgrace

Shelly's Ex-New Chap Revisited

His arm's back in plaster
His shed's in a state
He's got tools all over the landing
And he's calling you mate

He says he's a life coach
He's held together with matchsticks
He shaved his pubes with your razor
Left the dregs on your glass bricks

HMRC (Man Band)

A man band made up of walked over ex-husbands with
financial problems. Started out as Human Rug Mug's
Club, but then I noticed I got the initials in the wrong
order so I changed the name to Human Rubble Millets
Cuddle, but I had made the same mistake again, so they
are now known as Hug Me Rhona Cameron.

I'm Going Home (Outpatient Round)

I'm going home
I'm going home
To see my mom and nan
I'm going home

I'm going home
I'm going home
I'm going insane

Trying to Download the Whole Internet

(Plan for a Song / Inspiring Film Treatment.)

An adult lays alone in a dark, dingy bedroom; quiet but
for the background noise of extractor fans, town centre
traffic and bottle bins being emptied. Shaking his head,
he forces his way through a plate of baked beans. Black
T-shirt, trousers and socks still on from the previous
nights' work. Belongings in boxes and bin bags thrown
around the room and pushed over to the other side of
his double bed. No duvet, no linen;
Downloading the whole internet.

Slips into his automatic wake up routine; switches on
the TV and the computer screen. Swivels them around
to face him and continues to ignore the both of them.
Wireless key pad, wireless mouse, forever at his side
the helpless man quickly scans through the news sites.
Tired and crumpled over, depressed there is nothing
of interest. No world changing event, he rolls over.
Not even a celebrity break up, he rolls over;
Downloading the whole internet.

A dirty towel thrown over the curtain rail to block any
crack of light. Laying on the bed, he scratches his shins
to get rid of that slept in socks feeling. His socks come
off, tension in the room builds as if this is no regular
occurrence. The floor is ridden with old empty protein
shake wrappers and chewed up wads of paper. Picking
a scab on his elbow he says to himself 'I should have set
up a Facebook account when I had wavy hair and a tan'
and as soon as these words leave his mouth the loading

bar slowly edges over 0.4%;
Now, he's downloading the whole internet.

The hours are long, and the pay is shit. But, this man is
not like you because he is;
Downloading the whole internet.

It is a constantly uphill task. One day he will have it all.
One day he will be up to date. Salmon swim up river,
that Greek bloke pushed that rock, but this balding
man is all alone, sat in his underwear, in a makeshift
bedroom in his nan's house;
Downloading the whole internet.

Rank Slide Show (The Story of Nigel Jones, Prick)

He lost his licence for making love at the wheel, to
a lady on a motorbike in the neighbouring lane. A
slideshow of his demise is to be shown at the Grafte
Manor Hotel, Bromsgrove. Several hundred are expected to attend to gloat.

In the interest of clarity, I should mention this is a totally different Nigel Jones to the one who took Mom
out to dinner and ruined my school days.

Consoling Words

You have your whole life in front of you (crossed out)
You're young you have so much potential (crossed out)
You haven't killed anyone.

I Dearly Wish I Had Never Let You Put Your iPod Nano on During Sex

A TV show for couples whose relationships have been ruined by ill-timed personal headphone use.

Long Distance Lorry Driver Travelling Past His Home Mid-Journey on a Motorway to Many Miles Away

Six-hour journey
Sunlight makes me want to vomit
Very bad headache
Very bad headache, darling

Five hundred miles for some office stationery
Pull over for a garage pasty
Very bad headache
Very bad headache, darling

I saw you a few hours back
Another man leaving the house
Very bad headache
Very bad headache, darling

Feeling in my stomach won't leave me
Think I saw him carry your suitcase out from
    the pantry
Very bad headache
Very bad headache, darling

Just started pissing down with rain, the pavement is very slippy and dangerous.
12 February at 14:42

Bits of the jonny machine keep on falling off but I can't pick them up without dropping stuff.
12 February at 14:44

I don't know what the hell my legs are doing, but it isn't good.
12 February at 14:44

I'm soaked through, resting the machine on a bin. I'd like to go back in time and apologise to my younger self. This bin bloody stinks.
12 February at 14:51

A lady just took pity on me and picked up a bit of the machine that fell off when I was trying to get through the carousel doors to the precinct.
12 February at 14:56

I meant to say thank you but accidentally said I love you.
12 February at 14:57

Jesus Christ.
12 February at 14:58

I can feel my face has gone really red. Thank God nobody here knows me.
12 February at 14:59

I can never come back to Woking ever again.
12 February at 15:00

I will never come back to Woking ever again.
12 February at 15:01

I am carrying a 1950's solid metal condom machine through a packed out shopping precinct in broad daylight. Somehow part of me isn't even surprised this is what my life has come to now.
12 February at 15:03

I've just got to make it up to the top floor and

over to the car park
without dying.
12 February at 15:05

I can't die like this.
12 February at 15:06

If only I had the use of
my Slendertone these past
few months. Or even just
looked after myself for
my entire life up until
this point.
12 February at 15:07

If I died like this
I would never forgive
myself.
12 February at 15:07

I should have paid more
attention at school, mar-
ried young and lived off
the land.
12 February at 15:08

What the fuck have I been
doing all these years?
12 February at 15:10

Bloody practising my own
signature that's what.
12 February at 15:11

I am carrying a 1950's
solid metal condom mach-
ine through a shopping
precinct. This is not
something that a normal
person would do.
12 February at 15:24

Got such a stitch.
12 February at 15:25

This must be doing me
some form of good. If I'm
not dying then I must be
at least getting fit or
building muscle. I think
my arms are bleeding.
12 February at 15:19

On an escalator in a shopping centre and I don't
know why.
12 February at 15:29

In a lift crying
12 February at 15:32

The lift is made of glass.
12 February at 15:32

In the car park looking
for my mom, got no signal.
12 February at 15:44

Can't find Mom. I thought
I was coming to the end
of this shit, but it just
keeps on going and going.
12 February at 15:48

Think I was looking on
the wrong floor.
12 February at 15:56

Definitely was.
12 February at 16:03

And again.
12 February at 16:14

Getting panicky now.
12 February at 16:27

I think I've hit the wall.
12 February at 16:29

I have lost my mom.
12 February at 16:33

Maybe she left without me.
12 February at 16:44

Just seen Mom.
12 February at 16:51

Just been sick.
12 February at 16:58

In the car. Silence.
12 February at 17:03

Not even a hello.
12 February at 17:07

My arms kill and every-
thing is shaking. Mom's
doing 80 in a 30 zone.
12 February at 17:19

I have put myself through
a trauma here today.
I don't think my body
will recover from
this for weeks.
12 February at 17:43

Feeling sick again.
12 February at 17:50

Just realised I've gone
overdrawn again buying
that McDonald's earlier.
12 February at 17:53

Well I haven't just real-
ised, I knew it was going
to happen when I paid for
it but I was just taken
in by the whole service
station holiday feeling.
12 February at 17:55

What a waste. £30 charge
for going 30p over my
overdraft limit. Why the
hell did I go large?
12 February at 19:27

Mom's not talking to me
again. I have five days
to get £30 together or
I'm in deep shit.
12 February at 18:23

Jonny just rang and told
me, he's found a better
machine on the internet
in Newcastle.
12 February at 18:31

I don't even think he was
joking.
12 February at 18:39

He wasn't joking. Cannot
believe I've missed Hollyoaks for this.
12 February at 18:49

Just been sick on myself.
12 February at 18:58

Mom made out the Big Mac
and flipped her lid. She's
opened all the windows to
get rid of the sick smell.
I'm bloody freezing.
12 February at 19:17

So cold.
12 February at 19:27

Every time I leave the
house I seem to end up
vomiting. Just don't know
where it's going to end.
12 February at 19:51

It's got to stop.
12 February at 19:52

If I die before I'm 60 I
will be so miffed at the
hand I have been dealt
here today.
12 February at 20:58

Just secured a walk on
role in a leading TV soap.
12 February at 22:09

Sorry that was a lie.
12 February at 22:20

Going to watch Live Darts
in bed with my life, it's
on ITV4, good night.
12 February at 23:14

The Canteen 'Should Have Been'

(New TV show kind of like *Happy Days* but less happy
and set in Bromsgrove. Eight minute theme tune.)

Going down to soak me up some resentment
At the Canteen 'Should Have Been'
Going down for a lukewarm reception
At the Canteen 'Should Have Been'
The food is cold but the staff are colder
Only one place to go when you wake up older
The Canteen 'Should Have Been'

Going back in shit clothes
To the Canteen 'Should Have Been'
Going back with a stubbed toe
To the Canteen 'Should Have Been'
Where the walls all shake with badly aged drum beats
And the plates are all filled with mounds of cheap beef
The Canteen 'Should Have Been'

Where the worn out beauty searches for change
Where the one time singer loses her range
Where someone asks you for the time and you tell
    them, and they tell you to fuck off
Where the discredited librarian nurses a whooping
    cough
Where reheated stories are worn smooth of fact
Where people talk, but never act
From the offices of silent misery they traipse alone
To the place you go for dinner when you can't
    face home
The Canteen 'Should Have Been'

Open all hours except the ones you want
The Canteen 'Should Have Been'
Where the hairnet stifles the flattened bouffant
The Canteen 'Should Have Been'
Ask for sugar and they give you salt
A kick in the shin and a night in the vault
And it's always someone else's fault
At the Canteen 'Should Have Been'

Where the migraine meets the flickering light
Where the toothache greets the frozen shite
Where stale bread breeds a hardened crust
Where the specials are off and the vendors bust
Where comebacks are half-heartedly scrawled
    upon napkins
As bankrupts fleece the pockets of has-beens
Where troublesome pendulums swing overhead
Where every eye is black and every balance is red
It's the Canteen 'Should Have Been'

Where the mains all come with prepared excuses
Where pain is surplus and love is useless
Where the idle years leave an unquenchable thirst
Where those who've been last, all wait to be first
It's all yours at the Canteen 'Should Have Been'

Going back to stand in single file
At the Canteen 'Should Have Been'
Going back to stand on public trial
At the Canteen 'Should Have Been'
However you get there you've gone the wrong way
However long you've been there it's too long a stay
It's the Canteen 'Should Have Been'

Voice-over: *The Canteen 'Should Have Been'* is filmed in front of a mostly live studio audience.

[*Cue Action*]

The Last Phone Call (Marital Interference)

Wife: I can't hear you, what did you say? [*Interference*] The lines breaking up?

Man: What?

Wife: It's breaking up?

Man: [*Mishearing*] We're breaking up?

Wife: If you want to?

Man: [*Taken aback*] Is that what you want?

Wife: Okay.

Man: Okay?

Wife: Oh well. We had a good run...

Okay. Bye then.

Man: Bye.

The couple never spoke to each other ever again. That was that, the end of a marriage.

A Terribly Sad Story (Real Time Drama Like '24')

A man gets locked in the toilet for 28 years, and on his escape he actually prefers ITV coverage of the football. Starring Robson Greene.

Harmful Curtains (Like Twilight but with Centre Partings)

Teeny-bopper novel about a man with a curtains style haircut which takes on a life of its own to cause that man harm. Ideally, the whole thing should be based around the following line;

'Every time Philip tried to look forward past tomorrow the curtains closed.'

Doctors

Doctor: What seems to be the problem?
Patient: I don't know, I just don't feel on top of things much lately.
Doctor: Okay, what I'm going to ask you to do is join the club.

Off the Meds (Claritin Refrain)

Off the meds
Off the meds
Off the meds
Off the meds

To a Very Special Dual Carriageway Stroller (Load Baring Rucksack Full of Love)

Unfussy woman
Looks past societies hold ups
Dual carriageway stroller
Showered on the hard shoulder at Ruislip
Fleece full of fluids
Rucksack full of love
Shadowy past lovers
Load baring rucksack full of love

Dual carriageway stroller
Let's move to Hawaii
First thing t'morri morning
Decide we don't like it and come back

Shady past woman
My heart in your fingerless gloves
Take me where you are going
With your load baring rucksack full of love

Grown Man in a Paddling Pool (Film Theme)

Grown man in a paddling pool
With a look of concentration
Grown man in a paddling pool
Born under a bad constellation
The water started freezing, briefly turned warmer
And then went cold again
A moment's worth of pleasure
From a lifetime full of pain

//Grown Man in a Paddling Pool. Back garden motion picture.

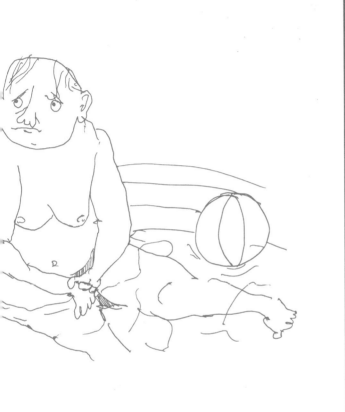

Fidget in a MRI Scan

The important thing you need to remember to enjoy this piece is that you are not allowed to move around or fidget during an MRI kidney scan, something I found out to my own cost.

Fly lands on your nose during an MRI scan
Feels like you might sneeze during an MRI scan
German Shepherd licks your face during an MRI scan
Some old chap's warm breath up close on the nape of
    your neck during an MRI scan
Third parties nasal hair trimmer rooting around your
    nostril during an MRI scan
Semi-defrosted chicken fillet dripping into your
    eyeball during an MRI scan
The entire contents of a compost bin emptied into
    your hair and trousers during an MRI scan
Fruit salad in your socks during an MRI scan
Fried egg down your leg during an MRI scan
Hamster in your armpit during an MRI scan
Shop bought onion bhajis placed individually between
    each one of your toes during an MRI scan
A smokers yellow nail clipping inserted deep in the
    recess of your belly button during an MRI scan
A hot electric light beaming directly onto your face
    during an MRI scan
Twelve thousand people tutting with every slight
    move you make during an MRI scan
Nurse looks up your gown and does that little pinky
    sign women sometimes make during an MRI scan
You swallow a tear and it gives you the hiccups during
    an MRI scan

Thursday

Man 1: Excuse me, what day is it?

Man 2: Please leave me alone.

Man 1: Yes, but what day is it?

Man 2: I don't know.

Man 1: Me neither. Feels like a Tuesday.

Man 2: I'm not sure.

Man 1: Do you reckon it could be Tuesday? Could be couldn't it?

Man 2: Maybe.

Man 1: Might be mightn't it?

Man 2: Yes.

Man 1: Yep, Could be.

Things We All Ought to Be Doing

Getting out and about.
Speaking properly.
Getting some new clothes.
Sorting our mobile phone contracts out once
and for all.

Thursday 22 February 2007

Just googled today's date
A certain smell is emanating from your face.
Come on man, it's getting boring.
(Idea for a song based on an email from my ex-wife.)

Soapstar for the 21st Century (Duffle Coated Man)

Not been without a chewing gum in his gob for 35
years. Wears a plastic bag for a vest. Named his daugh-
ter Diadora. His catchphrase is *'When I say Brita, you
say filter'*.

The Take That Documentary

Celebrity on a laptop
In black and white.
They have got coffee in a recyclable cup.
They are eating sushi with chopsticks and stuff
It's brilliant!
If you change the channel now I will be very upset
    with you.
They've got bottled water and grapes.
Soft focus shots backstage.
Eyes done with a laser.
T-shirt they don't need to pay for.
Haircut without asking
Make-up and a swimming pool back garden.
I would like a life like that
But I seldom leave the house.

Not in the Lounge Pal

I have heard something on the television
I have heard something on the television
I will now repeat verbatim
In your lounge
Budge up, shift over

The man knows everything about everything
Including home heating, tequila and the all important
   attacking wing back
I wish I was asleep on a Sunday morning of a bank
   holiday weekend, not even dreaming of anything

Dear extended family, friends and wider public;
You think I don't have a clue about anything
   but I do, I know about failure
Now, I am selling near enough half a tube of
   toothpaste on eBay, please show me your support
   and bid generously. Merry Christmas!   ●

I have heard something on the television
I have heard something on the television
I will now repeat verbatim
In your lounge
Budge up, shift over

The man knows everything about nothing
He can name the year of any song on *Top of the Pops 2*
   with solid conviction
I wish I was asleep on a Sunday morning of a bank
   holiday weekend, not even dreaming of anything
Taking paracetamol for a headache is not a flaw

Nan Don't Want No Gazpacho Mom

(Reggae Track)

Nan don't want no gazpacho Mom [x5]

Hyperventilating with Love (Catch My Breath)

Bring yourself to love me
Everybody gives up someday
I'll get a haircut when I'm able
I promise I'll do just what you say

Bring yourself to love me
Everybody takes their eye off the ball sometimes
I'll accept a decade is an exception
I'll find a phone contract you don't mind

Bring yourself to love me
I'm sure it will all be fine
In some unnamed date in the future
Anything beyond two weeks' time

Bring yourself to love me
I'll learn a foreign language
I'll find some better ancestors
I'll do something with my personality
Once I catch my breath

<u>Wesley Henry's Facebook</u>

I've just woken up. Really
tired. Slept in the port-
akabin again.
16 March at 08:48

Trying not to be too hard
on myself. It's just one
of those things.
16 March at 09:56

Having some really dark
thoughts here. Every time
I sleep in the portakabin
I wake up with my hand in
a bowl of water.
16 March at 10:22

Spent all morning trying
to keep my eyes slightly
out of focus so as not
to notice any of my imme-
diate surroundings.
16 March at 11:14

I always think I can do
life properly when it's
night time but when I
wake up and it's light
everything seems a lot,
lot harder.
16 March at 11:20

Spent all night thinking
how I am going to change
everything in my entire
life. Woke up bloody
knackered.
16 March at 11:22

Already slightly bored of
everything I wanted to
achieve last night, done
it all in my head a mil-
lion times over now. It's
bloody boring man.
16 March at 11:45

Ran myself down into the
ground with hope. Woke
up in a portakabin, wet
through. It's always just
so disappointing.
16 March at 11:53

44 next year.
16 March at 12:01

Basically nearly fifty.
16 March at 12:03

Got the bank up my ass, I
need to find £30 by Friday
or things could spiral
well out of my control.
16 March at 12:12

I'm working a sixty hour
week and not even close to
breaking even. Essentially
the problem is I'm not
being paid whatsoever.
16 March at 12:16

Can't think straight when
it's light. Everything is
just so bright, it's like
watching a big HD TV in
PC World but watching a
really shit programme.
16 March at 12:19

A totally immersive experience is okay for a vast
rainforest or something
exotic but a makeshift
bed in a portakabin floor
just takes the piss.
16 March at 12:21

Feels like I'm in an East-
enders drug plot here but
I have never even touched
drugs. I never got past
how Nan would react.
16 March at 12:23

Living the life of a drug
junkie is even more dep-
ressing for a 100% T-total

person. It's bloody rel-
entless, there is no
temporary high, just
Tetris on my phone and
a wet sleeping bag.
16 March at 12:25

Got to get back home to
my proper bed.
16 March at 13:40

Back at Nan's house. Just
spent three hours in my
wardrobe trying to think
things through. Need it
to be night time again.
16 March at 15:52

My finances would be per-
fectly manageable if I
could just get paid.
16 March at 16:48

Got to ask for a meeting
with Jonny tomorrow, del-
iver him a full business
plan for a £30 loan, bare
minimum.
16 March at 16:59

Got my suit on already for
tomorrow, already feel
quite nervous. Just found

some bad memories in one
of the trouser pockets.
16 March at 19:12

I'm going to go to sleep
early tonight, no phone,
no computer, no music,
no nothing. Got to be
fresh for tomorrow.
16 March at 20:39

Terrible night. Couldn't
get to sleep for ages,
too much cold hard real-
ity. Woke up in a sweaty
panic, my suit's a stale
smelling bloody mess.
17 March at 08:43

Hiding in the car park
waiting for the right
moment to confront Jonny.
17 March at 09:44

I texted him about the
meeting earlier and he's
cleared out one of the
portakabins and put five
random chairs in there.
17 March at 09:48

Just seen some bloke turn
up with two video cameras

and it looks like Jonny's
invited everyone he knows
to look through the win-
dow. They all have £30
laid out on their tables.
17 March at 10:16

It's on Facebook. 'Dragon's
Den Pitch, Wesley Henry
pitches ideas to local
business mogul Mr.Jonny
Sheaths hoping for a lump
sum cash injection. The
more the merrier.'
17 March at 10:24

He must have got wind of
my cash request off Mom
or Nan.
17 March at 10:36

Keep on sneaking a peak
around the corner from
behind someone's people
carrier. There's bloody
loads of people there now.
At least 14 on last count.
17 March at 11:14

Why am I always hiding
from the past, the present
or the future?
17 March at 11:22

Bloody Jonny all over this is. Getting me to publicly jump through hoops for £30 which he technically already owes me, and more.
17 March at 11:29

I'm a fully grown man, I can do this. I just need an idea.
17 March at 11:23

100% Biodegradable Organic Vegan Condoms.
17 March at 11:42

Permanent Condoms.
17 March at 11:42

Semi permanent condoms.
17 March at 11:43

Sports Condoms.
17 March at 11:44

A condom that takes your pulse rate.
17 March at 11:44

Every time we sell a condom we donate one to a school kid.
17 March at 11:46

Every time we sell a condom we donate one to a school kid in Africa.
17 March at 11:46

A condom with an extension/mirror on the end that makes your penis look roomier to potential buyers/occupants.
17 March at 11:48

Got to be something condom related else he won't bite. That or scrap metal.
17 March at 11:51

100% Biodegradable Condoms won't wash, Jonny puts his condoms all around the duck pond in Morton Stanley Park for free local advertising.
17 March at 11:53

Feel like praying to God.
17 March at 11:54

I need some form of holy miracle here. Got to get out of this somehow. I have had enough now.
17 March at 11:55

I'm going over.
17 March at 11:57

I can't go over.
17 March at 11:58

I went over.
17 March at 12:03

I can't do this.
17 March at 12:08

On the floor of the car
park. Feel like I have
just been hit by a ton
of bricks. There's a big
crowd of people around me.
I can't stop saying sorry.
17 March at 12:13

Every time I try to talk
the muscles in the cor-
ner of my mouth start
violently shaking.
17 March at 12:16

I am in the arena. Jonny
says I have to pitch an
idea to him because all
these people are here now.
Everything in my body
feels wrong.
17 March at 12:18

I don't really want to
make my financial situa-
tion publicly known.
17 March at 12:21

I haven't got a clue what
I am going to say. The
well is dry. The locker
is empty.
17 March at 12:22

Jonny stole all my best
ideas years ago.
17 March at 12:24

I have no one to turn to
and he bloody well knows
it. Banks won't touch me.
I've got nothing.
17 March at 12:24

Why has everything got to
be a pitch nowadays?
17 March at 12:25

I tell you what if this
goes well with Jonny today
I'm never pitching to go
to the toilet ever again.
17 March at 12:26

I think it's my turn to
speak next. I can't stop

shaking and ruing lots of
different days.
17 March at 12:29

Fuck this I am going to
file for bankruptcy.
17 March at 12:31

Think I might be having a
stroke, but it may just be
wishful thinking.
17 March at 12:33

I have got blood all over
my hands and my face but
I don't know where it's
coming from.
17 March at 12:35

Really unideal preparation
this is.
17 March at 12:37

I don't know what to go
with. Think it's going
to have to be the Sports
Condoms, it's shit but
it's all I've got.
17 March at 12:38

Good God what just happ-
ened back there?
17 March at 13:12

Jonny just kept on saying
'People just want to hump'
over and over. It really
threw me.
17 March at 13:18

I think the blood on my
face put me off, I could
hardly speak.
17 March at 13:24

Seem to have come out
owing Jonny even more
money than I did before.
17 March at 13:26

I'm £1500 in the red. My
finances are in turmoil
yet again. I've fucked it.
17 March at 13:32

I have nothing left to
sell. All I have is a
smart phone that I am
locked in to and fills
me with the deepest regret
every time I touch it.
17 March at 13:34

I still remember when I
had a wife and a house.
17 March at 13:36

What I Have Learned From Life

If you are shy and anxious, you will have a shit life.

It's probably best to have a good childhood and be talented. Sow your seed for a few years, fall in love at twenty, settle down, marry when you're twenty-five and then have perfect children.

Don't waste your time having a dig at boy bands, pop stars or TV presenters. They are having much more fun and a lot more sex than you. Leave them be and spend your time doing things that will make people want to have sex with you.

Try and figure out what you want to do with your life before you begin to think 'it's too late for me, I'll concentrate on my children'.

It's nice to have a good, warm coat and shoes that y● are at peace with.

Don't bother illegally downloading music or searching for cover art. Get a career and a well-rounded lifestyle and you'll have more than enough disposable income to fund a music collection.

I have found it is best not to be friends with, or have any type of association with, people who play any sort of computer games.

Never ever keep Coca-Cola on your bedside table.

Social Skills

The most important thing
In the entire universe
Social skills
Social skills

Social skills Peter
Social skills John
Social skills Stephen
Social skills Ron
Social skills

No one in their right mind can underplay the inherent
    importance of social skills
The best thing since fresh air, sliced bread and hot
    water bottles
It's a basic common courtesy Carol
It's just social skills

Social skills Sarah
Social skills Shanice
Social skills Kelly
Social skills Denise
Social skills

The most interesting thing
In the known universe
Social skills
Social skills
I do worry about you honey, I do, into the early hours
I do worry about you honey, and your table manners
It's just social skills darling, social skills

Spray Paint the Free Barclays Pens Gold and Sell Them Online for £20 a Pop (Pitch)

Semi-profitable business run alongside the deluxe IKEA pencil and executive Argos pen with free chain ranges.

Sad but True (Appraisal of a Man's Life Story)

Sad but true.
The phrase you just cannot shake off
When you leave the room
And talk turns to you.

I'm not sure they know you're at the door listening
But the subject did come up.

If You Are Down (Heartfelt Love Song)

If you are down
Try having something to eat
If you are down
Maybe go for a swim
If you are down
Please think twice before involving me

[*The song now ventures into a spoken word bit like on 'Oh Carol' by Neil Sedaka.*]

You see darling I'm too sympathetic for my own good.
I feel your pain, and whilst you'll be back up and about
in a few days, I'll drag myself down to your level but

then when you get better I'll go down further and further. So, darling, if you're feeling down, please at least give it a couple of weeks before involving me. [*Sax solo*] I lost December because you had a bad dinner at the two-for-one.

[*Angelic backing singers swoon and a hot plate sizzles.*]

If you are down
I'd like to say I'd pick you up
If you are down
But I don't have a car
If you are down
And I can't drive

Mr. Trumpet Nose (Concerto Nolberto)

Mr. Trumpet Nose is a normal man but when he blows his nose it sounds like a trumpet. Often his sneezes come at the most inopportune moment.

Idea for a sketch that can just be repeated in different locations and scenarios;

Mr. Trumpet nose goes to the cinema.
       ″   ″   ″   ″   to the library.
       ″   ″   ″   ″   to war.

Fighting the Inevitability of Bullshit

Four hours and then I gave up.

Wesley Henry's Dream (Is Over)

Sit yourself in front of the music channel
   and stay there for eight days
Invite the nearest dickhead over for dinner
Learn his opinions and adopt his ways
Cos the dream is over
A tortured odd job man is just a tortured man

Take yourself down the tip
   and bring every film I ever made
The VHS format is defunct
The final act has been played
The dream is over
A tortured odd job man is just a tortured man

And what's the difference between a tortured genius
   and just some odd bloke on the bus? (A blow job?)
And who decides what's the difference between a
   tortured genius and some odd bloke on the bus?
   (A bunch of blow jobs?)

Bring that big old list of things I said I'd do
Place it into the hands of my every enemy
Any hope I had has gone
Any pride is just a memory
Because the dream is over

Fixing a sink does not require a week on the brink
   and an evening of poetry
Fixing a sink does not require a full-time shrink
   and a weekend of woe-is-me
A tortured odd job man is just a tortured man

Finding Yourself is Bullshit (Orienteering Show)

Spent the best part of £5,000 trying to find yourself.
Got a glimpse and then spent another £10,000 trying
to lose yourself. We've all been there. I have found
in life it's easier trying to find other people, or better
still, places. Welcome to *Finding Yourself is Bullshit,*
the lifestyle and orienteering show with a twist.

Davey Two Balls (Comedy Show)

New show based all around the boy who used to bring
the ball to school for break and lunchtime. He was the
sort of lad who had a protractor for anybody. Anyway,
he's all grown up now and doesn't have a fixed abode.
But, still he's always down the park trying to start a
game up with his coat full of stuff he hopes people
might want to borrow.

He wears bin bags for shoes because he has lent out
each and every pair of astro trainers he has ever had.
By night he secretly tends to the local playing fields.
By day he roams the streets mumbling to himself.
His catchphrases include:

> Fair does.
> Next goal wins.
> Anyone up for headers and volleys.
> Rush keeper or stick.
> Just tek it.
> Wun't using it anyway.
> Want a bite?

'Davey Two Balls' and his big overcoat of possibility. //

// *The Last Poor Sod, Artist's Impression of.*

A Hollywood Blockbuster II (The Last Poor Sod)

The Start:
Something awful happens.

The Middle:
I see a specialist who puts me on a six month intensive
programme to rebuild my life.

The End:
The six month programme takes eighteen months and
the results are hit and miss. I have good and bad days.

[*Post-script: Loads more crap happens.*]

The Nearly Man

Written as a direct counterpoint to the universal winner's anthem 'Champione, Champione, Ole, Ole, Ole'.

The Nearly Man
Forever popping his pants back on in a blush
A front row seat to watch the opportunities pass by

Nearly had a happy marriage
Nearly had a house
Nearly had a film career
Nearly had his health

Finally had a breakdown and moved in with his nan
Who's that their Mommy?
That's the Nearly Man

Half his head cut off the photograph in the local paper
Half his name misspelt on his certificate for good
    behaviour
All his effort spent, half of it wasted
All his needles lent to the bottom of a hay shed
That's the Nearly Man

Forever sitting in Argos waiting for his number to
    come up
A front row seat to watch all the other happy customers
    go home

The ugly duckling, who became the ugly duck
The fairy tale frog who got squashed to fuck

Wallet full of gift vouchers expired or not eligible in
    this country
Joy one centimetre out of his reach in every direction
Never the right place to put his...perfection

Destined to be
Disappointed to have been
The Nearly Man

Summer Holidays / Dreams / Career / Life / Saturday Night

We thought we were going to do something brilliant
but in the end we didn't do anything at all.

Never doing public speaking ever again.
17 March at 14:02

Don't know what I'm doing man, the only thing really keeping me going is the promise of future advances in technology.
17 March at 14:08

Got to hold out for a time in the future when everything is done on a computer. A virtual reality perfect life like the Matrix but easier to understand and set in Bromsgrove or Redditch.
17 March at 14:11

I think I am still bleeding from somewhere. Mom's going to go mad if I've ruined my best shirt.
17 March at 14:14

Can't spend another Mother's Day just apologising. It's depressing when your previous Google search history is just various failed attempts at hard to spell words to say sorry.
17 March at 14:38

43 years is long enough to wait for your life to start, but it's a really hard habit to break.
17 March at 14:42

Having quite a bit of trouble walking here.
17 March at 14:47

Slumped on the side of a road. Think I might've been run over.
17 March at 15:16

Think it was before I did the pitch.
17 March at 15:18

I have a load of carbon fibre stuck in my ass and I can't move my left arm.
17 March at 15:33

It's quite hard to pick carbon fibre out your ass without getting beeped at.
17 March at 15:37

Evrythin isgo ing bblack.
17 March at 15:45

Woke up in the hospital.
I actually feel quite re-
assured to be here. I'm
in the right place. I'm
in the right place.
18 March at 12:06

Trying to piece together
what exactly happened to
me. Specifically yesterday.
18 March at 12:42

Just found out I got run
over before the pitch by
the people carrier I was
hiding behind. I didn't
real⬤ take it in at
the time because I was
too nervous about the
presentation.
18 March at 13:02

I have broken my arm and
leg and sustained quite
heavy blows to the head
and ass.
18 March at 13:06

It's quite nice lying in
bed at past two in the

afternoon with absolutely
no guilt whatsoever.
18 March at 13:26

The more fucked up you
are in this place the
more people respect you.
It's great. I think I
have found my Graceland.
18 March at 14:02

Jonny's just turned up
with some tracksuited
lawyer he sells vids to.
He just keeps on shouting,
'Bingo time!' and rub-
bing his hands together.
18 March at 16:16

They reckon I'm liable
for a big payout if I do
what they say. I was quite
happy just with the lay
down, this is beyond my
wildest dreams.
18 March at 16:22

Jonny settled out of court
for five grand.
18 March at 16:53

Apparently he knew the
guy who ran me over and

he didn't want any fuss.
This is fantastic.
18 March at 17:52

Feels a bit strange rec-
eiving insurance money in
a carrier bag. Plus I'm
sure I saw Jonny with two
bags when he got out his
car, not just one.
18 March at 18:08

Couldn't face another
day in court after the
divorce though and at
least I can afford to buy
Mom a belated Mother's
Day present now.
18 March at 17:58

For the first time in a
decade I can honestly say
life is turning my way.
Once I get my arm and leg
out of plaster there will
be no stopping me.
18 March at 19:43

Going to be a proper
actor now, no more condom
bullshit. No more Mother's
Days in hospital.
18 March at 19:49

I woke up this morning,
stepped outside the front
door and enjoyed a mom-
ent's breath of fresh
air without a single bad
memory to tie around it.
This is the life.
19 March at 07:49

Just rubbing a mint tea
bag on my face. I feel
like a king!!
18 March at 10:22

Someone from Orange just
phoned and I was so rel-
axed it felt like I was
on holiday from my actual
self, it was unbelievable!
18 March at 11:12

I can only imagine this
is what it must feel like
to be an actual grown up
human being.
18 March at 11:20

The sky today is beau-
tiful.
18 March at 11:44

Since I've had my arm in
plaster nobody expects

me to do anything, they
treat me like a King. I
can see the old form of
pity shifting over for a
far more positive version.
18 March at 12:02

Once my arms and legs get
fixed up I think I will
start getting fit and eating properly. It's time
to start doing things the
right way for once.
18 March at 12:14

Called a meeting with Jon,
going to tell him I am
letting him go, I need a
proper agent.
18 March at 12:22

There is no room in show-
biz for a man who publicly
sprays his balls with
Airwick mid-chat.
18 March at 12:22

It's for the best, life is
short and I have to make
the most of it. It's time
that fat prick got his
comeuppance.
18 March at 12:41

Just come out the meeting,
think it went well.
18 March at 14:38

Jonny has convinced me
the best way to make my
name as an actor is to
bring out a paperback
book. He says all the big
names have them.
18 March at 14:42

He says he can get me a
good deal at the moment
because he is getting
his business advice one
printed as well. I think
it's some form of two-for-
one deal. The rough costs
work out at exactly five
grand Jonny says.
18 March at 14:48

I've got to keep on tell-
ing myself this is going
to work out.
18 March at 14:56

I really hope this is
going to work out.
18 March at 15:14

Dinner

WH: Wesley Henry
PM: Pizza Man

[*Phone rings.*]

PM: Hello, Carl's Pizza. How can I help you?

WH: Hello, can I have my dinner?

PM: Sorry?

WH: What's for dinner?

PM: I don't know what you mean mate.

WH: I just want my dinner.

PM: Well what do you want to order?

WH: I don't know, just my dinner.

PM: This is a take-away restaurant pal.

WH: What?

PM: Tell me what you want?

WH: I want my dinner.

PM: Do you want Margarita pizza? Hawaiian?

WH: Ye, fine whatever.

PM: Okay. Medium or large?

WH: Whatever you're having. What time's dinner?

PM: It's about a twenty-five-minute wait?

WH: No.

PM: Pardon?

WH: I need to watch my programmes.

PM: Well what time do you want to pick it up?

WH: Dinner time.

PM: Just say a time, we shut at ten.

WH: Just leave mine on the side I will reheat it in the microwave later.

PM: Okay, that will be £4.50 on collection?

WH: No.

PM: Pardon?

WH: Yes.

PM: Okay? Can I take a name?

WH: No.

PM: Pardon?

WH: What?

PM: Can I take your name?

WH: No, not really.

PM: Well we need a name to place the order.

WH: You slept with my wife.

PM: What?

WH: You slept with my wife.

PM: Who?

WH: Shelly.

PM: I don't know any Shelly.

WH: You do. You had sex with Shelly.

PM: Not me sir.

WH: Yes you sir, you had sex with my wife.

PM: No.

WH: Yes mate, I saw you.

PM: Where?

WH: On Shelly.

PM: Where?

WH: Round the back of Smash N Grab.

PM: Nah, not me pal?

WH: Yes, you pal.

PM: No, it wasn't.

WH: Why lie?

PM: It really wasn't me.

WH: Don't lie.

PM: Sir, it was not me.

WH: Don't lie.

PM: I'm hanging up.

WH: That's it run away.

PM: If I ever get a call off this number again I will ring the police.

WH: I don't think you will.

PM: Why?

WH: You have a large birthmark on your lower right ass cheek.

PM: What?

WH: You heard. You have a large birthmark on your lower ass and you shagged my wife eight years ago in Smash N Grab's staff car park.

PM: How?... I don't know, what do you want?

WH: I want my dinner mate.

PM: What?

WH: I want my dinner and Shelly's not here to watch me make it anymore, so you are going to make it because you don't want your wife finding out about your little dalliances in car parks.

PM: Okay, okay, whatever you want.

WH: I want my life back. I want my wife back but you can't fix that can you pal cos she's got a new chap scratching her back now. So I want my dinner and I want it ready after my programmes finish.

PM: Okay.

WH: And I want it on a proper plate and I want you to cook it and wash it up.

PM: I can do that, I can do that. Anything, you just can't tell my wife.

WH: And I want employee discount on my order.

PM: But...

WH: But nothing. I want the 10% off.

PM: Okay, okay.

WH: I will collect my dinner after my programmes and then I don't want to ever see you again.

PM: What do you mean? I've got kids, my family...

WH: Shut up, you have lost me as a customer, I will never use your shop again.

PM: Okay, okay, okay.

WH: Now you better start getting my dinner ready.

PM: Okay, okay, can I just take a name?

WH: Forget the name, pal.

PM: How will I know it's you?

WH: Leave my food on the side like I said dickhead and don't get smart. Do you think I want to be making this phone call? Do you think I'm enjoying this any more than you?

PM: I'm sorry, I'm sorry.

WH: And if you ever speak to anyone about this call, I have an email ready in my drafts just waiting to be sent to the editor of the Vindicator requesting a full page advert telling everybody in the town about your grubby little love life.

PM: Okay.

WH: All I have to do is click send pal.

PM: Okay. I won't, I won't.

WH: I know you won't. I will leave the £4.05 on the counter in a brown envelope on pick up and leave the dirty plate on the step tomorrow morning.

PM: Okay, okay.

WH: Now cook my dinner and don't be expecting a tip. Just one click pal, remember, just one click, that is all.

PM: Okay.

WH: Okay… Bye then.

PM: Bye.

WH: Go then.

PM: Pardon?

WH: Go now.

PM: Okay. Bye.

WH: Bye

PM: Bye now.

WH: Okay bye…. Hang up then now.

PM: Okay. Bye. [*Hangs up.*]

WH: Bye.

3.

DATING PROFILE

Dating Profile

Within reason, this book has remained on quite a professional note up until this point. However, seeing as I am paying out my own pocket for this publication, Nan has persuaded me it does make business sense to include my dating profile, just in case. You never know who may be reading this thing. If one person were to like this book, and it just so happened that they were a heterosexual female, I would hate to think of them not being able to have the chance of settling down with me for life.

Certain people may think that putting your own dating profile in a book of a professional nature is a little pathetic, but I prefer to see it as a belt and braces approach to finding employment and love; killing two birds with one stone if you will. Anyway, I really can't afford to be out of work and alone for much longer so just do me a favour and go easy on me.

For those of you of the male sex, or of the happily married women variety, I suggest you read this section as a kind of celebrity interview like those you get in Sunday newspaper supplements. For those of you reading this book purely from a business mindset, why not imagine the following pages as an extended recruitment questionnaire.

// *Kicking back in some of my finest wedding / funeral attire.*

Dating Information

Age: 43.

Relationship Status: Betrayed.

Children: None.

Personality: Civil.

Appearance: Large bulbous head. More to love.
Outlook: Disappointed.

Location: Bromsgrove.　　　**Interests:** Limited.

Entertainment: Home movies / the internet.
Sports: I once met Julian Joachim at a charity do.

Bio: Actor / odd job man.
　　　Will be buff by Christmas.
　　　Looking for a gentle understanding lady.
　　　Not really too bothered about a sense of humour.
　　　Interested even sight unseen.

In My Own Words

The one thing I am most passionate about:
Changing the past.

The five things which I am most thankful for:
In no apparent order:

- Sleep.
- The internet.
- My PC / DVD player.
- My wireless mouse / keyboard combo.
- Having enough hot water for a bath.
  (All I need now is someone to share them with.)

My best life skills are:
Hindsight and the recognition and taking on of other people's problems.

My best personal quality is:
I will never give up on a failing relationship, no matter what the circumstances.

The most important quality I am looking for in another person is:
Lack of ambition or shopping around for a better offer to the point of being reckless in their devotion.

I typically spend my leisure time:
On the internet. Otherwise, ideally I like low key activities such as watching a film or going to the toilet. Anything that doesn't involve crowds and allows me plenty of thinking time to lament past behaviour.

Question & Answer

What makes you happy?
Very little. Maybe a good, warm tracksuit trouser.

When did you last cry, and why?
This morning, no real reason.

What is your greatest fear?
That I have already had my prime.

What is your greatest achievement?
Having full sex with a woman.

Trawling through the wreckage of love gone wrong. //

// *On the swing. In the park. Lamenting.*

// Out in the cold trying to be whoever you want me to be.

What was the last book that you read? What was it about? What did you like most about it?

It was called *Woulda, Coulda, Shoulda: Overcoming Regrets, Mistakes and Missed Opportunities* by Dr. Arthur Freeman and Rose DeWolf. It was a self-help book about dealing with regret which I am awfully ashamed to say I didn't finish.

What or who was the greatest love of your life?

A girl who cut my hair in Solihull once and kept on accidentally rubbing her tits up against me.

If you could bring something extinct back to life, what would you choose?

Blockbuster, pre drop-off bin.

If you could have a superpower, what would it be?

I would like a woman to hold my hand.

What has been your biggest disappointment?

The past ten years.

How would you like to be remembered?

Through some form of a bench or statue outside of my old Blockbuster store.

Who would you invite to your dream dinner party?

The girl from Solihull who cut my hair.

Is there any additional information you would like your matches to know about you?

I suspect I have several mental illnesses, but if you just keep your nose out there is no reason at all why they should cause you any bother.

//On a lilo, in a puddle, by the waste ground. Waiting for your call.

Love Applicants

Anybody interested in falling deeply in love with me should act quickly to get in there before any form of success arrives. Although at the moment I really have nothing to offer you, I am liable to be living quite a different life once people come to their senses and realise my true place in the world.

Life is a struggle trying to get Hollywood roles out of your nan's house in Bromsgrove. I am a perfectionist, most days found in unwashed pyjamas, on a crumb covered, broken office chair sighing. With enough effort though, on a good day, wearing my best clothes and in the right lighting conditions, I could be viewed in some people's eyes as a success with minimal Photoshop editing. How? International recognition.

As with all matters of the heart, prior to eminence, I will be working off a first come first serve basis. For ease of access, however, I would initially favour applicants residing within the Bromsgrove and Redditch area, ideally Stoke Pound. To book a date with me please head over to my dating webpage:

Date@8:
https://sites.google.com/site/dateateight/wesley-henry

Whilst still writing this book it is hard to judge future interest in me, but minibus pick ups could hypothetically be arranged should there be sufficient clamour. In the short term, Mom will be able to cater for dates of all dietary persuasions here at our shared living accommodation within Nan's house. I will also chip in what I can for any future dates outside of the home.

Everything I have to offer you, at home in my office/bedroom. //

// Potential spouses please ignore the following section.

4.

APOLOGIES

Sincere Apologies

Well that's it then, the end of the book. Congratulations if you have read the whole thing. I hope it was worth it. I had to take over six months off work to make this piece of crap and have pushed myself to the very edge of a full on mental breakdown in the process. I wish I had never bloody started the thing to be honest, but it's done now isn't it guys.

Since I have finished the book now, and I can't imagine I will ever put myself through making another one, I thought this was as good a chance as any to issue some apologies and air some long festering grievances.

First off, I would like to apologise to myself as I promised myself I would never get this low ever again.

Now for the grievances. I kept a list of these throughout the book making process.

- This book was a total ball ache to make.

- I gave myself piles for this shit.

- I have spent six months beating the crap out of myself to finish a book no one will ever give one shit about.

- This book will be sitting around for years as a memorial to bad advice and lost hope as I slide further and further down the social ladder.

- I put all my life and effort into this hunk of junk and I bet only about four people will read it.

- I've gone too far off kilter this time. This was my last big break, I am never going to get an out of court insurance payment like that ever again.

- I told Jonny that I couldn't fill a book and all I wanted to do was get on television, but he said to just write down all of my insecurities as he wanted to publish them for other people's entertainment. 'Mis lit sells Wes, just show them your deepest most inner most feelings', 'don't hold back'. I can honestly say this is the worst two for one deal I have ever been involved in.

- This book is just ammo for my ex-wife. I just don't see what it's all got to do with my acting.

- I have made a book about my life in Bromsgrove but if any-one in Bromsgrove reads this thing I will be finished.

- If I don't get an acting job or a wife out of this book, God knows how I'm going to put a positive spin on this period of my life. I'm going to be dragging this albatross around my neck for the next twenty years or more. Of that I am positively certain.

- Who the fuck reads books to hire actors?

//*Above space intentionally left blank for future complaints.*

More Apologies

To save some space on all future outgoing birthday, Christmas and Mother's Day cards I would like to publicly apologise here to my mom for a catalogue of issues dating back across several decades. Sorry also to my nan for all the swear words, sullying of the family name and questionable content within this book.

Next up, sorry to you the reader for any grammatical or spelling errors left uncorrected in this book. I did send the final transcript to a proofreader, but she thought the whole thing was just a long winded cry for help and refused to be involved in the project / my demise. Unfortunately, by the time she pulled out it was too late to get anyone else in and Jonny said that spelling is for fannies anyway.

Sorry also to any people who I have sent this book to through the post as a promotional tool, you didn't ask for this shit.

Sorry for anyone who has to pretend they like the thing whilst in a room with me (mainly Mom and Nan again).

Sorry again to my younger self.

Sorry for anyone who is the same position as me for not showing a success story of how to get out of this situation.

Sorry to Paul McKenna for being such a poor example of his self-improvement methods.

And finally, a general sorry for anyone I have missed out, barring Jonny Sheaths and my ex-wife Shelly, unless she will take me back.

Index

In Memoriam

During the making of this book we sadly lost Nan's Rover 200. Good bye old girl and thank you for the memories. You shall be dearly missed.

About This Book

A Life in Film and Bromsgrove was written in a frantic rush of impending doom, claustrophobia and anxiety; holed up in an upstairs study/bedroom at my nan's house, flogging a dead horse on a dodgy old copy of Microsoft Word.

Whilst making this book I took a sabbatical from Twitter and Facebook just to try to get something done for once in my life. Sadly, in that time I now learn I have lost both Rick Edwards from *T4* and Kinga from *Big Brother 6* as followers. Anyone still reading this junk, I beg you to please put your personal feelings to one side and follow me as it is good for my confidence.

Twitter:
@WesleyHenry1

Facebook:
www.facebook.com/WesleyHenryHead

I also like to write on YouTube comments pages here:

YouTube:
WesleyHenryHead

Anyone from Trading Standards please follow my agent on Twitter via @MrJonnySheaths, or by searching any one of the following tags:

#OldFatNeck
#SpinalComplaintsFromPoundingWronguns
#OldStickyFingers
#BogBotherer
#FullSexInAWheelyBin

Designed by Eight Years

Published by Eight Years Too Late

Copyright © Eight Years 2013

Eight Years assert the moral right to be identified as the authors of this work
in accordance with the Copyright, Designs and Patents Act 1988.

Picture Credits:

pg. 3 (Hunk) Adapted from © Anna Gunselman

pg. 17 (Fat Man) Adapted from © Mikael Häggström

pg. 19 (Dressing Gown) Adapted from © Contains Mild Peril

pg. 20 (Contortionist) Adapted from © Ron Dwight

pg. 35 (Pixelated Image) © Stallio

pg. 36 (Insects in the House) © Lee J Haywood

A CIP catalogue record for this book is available from the British Library.

Printed by Chapter Press

www.chapterpress.co.uk

First print run of 1,000 copies.

ISBN 978-0-9576521-0-1

Also available in electronic book.

www.eightyears.co.uk